The Last Bard

MAZ EVANS

A MESSAGE FROM CHICKEN HOUSE

When some superfamous Shakespearean characters come out of Will's grandfather's old book of plays and wreak havoc, you know you're in for some hilarious and heart-warming comedy. But I especially love Maz Evans because her bestselling stories reveal much more than just laughs, with some lovely truths about friendship, family and standing up for what's right. A bit like Shakespeare, really!

BARRY CUNNINGHAM
Publisher
Chicken House

The Last Bard

MAZ EVANS

Chicken House

2 PALMER STREET, FROME,
SOMERSET BA11 1DS

First published in the UK in 2025
Chicken House
2 Palmer Street
Frome, Somerset BA11 1DS
United Kingdom
www.chickenhousebooks.com

Chicken House/Scholastic Ireland, 89E Lagan Road, Dublin Industrial Estate,
Glasnevin, Dublin D11 HP5F, Republic of Ireland

For safety or quality concerns:
UK: www.chickenhousebooks.com/productinformation
EU: www.scholastic.ie/productinformation

Cover and interior design by Ali Al Amine
Typeset by Dorchester Typesetting Group Ltd

ISBN 978-93-5954-050-4

Printed in India at Acme Print O Pac.Pvt. Ltd. Noida.
This reprint edition: September 2025

A CIP catalogue record for this book is available from the British Library.

For my beloved friend

Tim Sutton

Lord, what fools we mortals be . . .

Also by Maz Evans

Who Let the Gods Out?
Simply the Quest
Beyond the Odyssey
Against All Gods

Oh Maya Gods!
Oh Mummy Mia!
Oh What a Knight!

Vi Spy: Licence to Chill
Vi Spy: Never Say Whatever Again
Vi Spy: The Girl with the Golden Gran

And for younger readers
The Exploding Life of Scarlett Fife
The Wobbly Life of Scarlett Fife
The Stormy Life of Scarlett Fife

CHAPTER I

The Summer's Tale

None of us knows where we are in our story. Today might be the start of a new tale, the end of one already told, or simply another chapter along its way. Our stories are often comedies, occasionally tragedies, many are histories and most are all three. Maybe we'll have to fight the monsters beyond. Or perhaps we must battle the beast within. We can never know how our stories will end, or even if they've already begun.

But for William Davenant, this story started in a traffic jam on the M3.

'Urgh,' Will groaned, pulling at the collar of his jumper for the thirtieth time in two hours, unsure if he was releasing the August heat from his body, or letting more in. 'It's soooo hot.'

'I'm sorry, kiddo,' his mother Mary apologized, aggressively twiddling a dial to improve the weak gasp of warm breath leaking from the fans. 'Uncle Claude said he'd get the air con fixed . . . Why don't you take your jumper off, you daft brush? You must be hotter than a dragon's vindaloo!'

'It's not your fault,' Will interrupted, not wanting his mum to feel bad. 'Uncle Claude says he'll do a lot of things.'

'He most certainly does,' Mary muttered, giving up and slamming her hand back on the steering wheel. The car inched forward on the shimmering tarmac. Will peered across the ocean of cars ahead, but still couldn't see any land. He returned to the sketch pad on his lap, adding wings to his drawing of their car as he imagined it taking off over the traffic and soaring towards the sea. Will liked to draw the world as he wanted it to be. The real picture before him didn't always make great viewing.

'We'll be there soon enough,' Mary promised, as she had done for the last hour in the sweltering, stationary traffic. 'And let's look on the bright side – we get a few days by the seaside! You'll love Arden Heights – our first proper holiday in years!'

'Cleaning out your dead dad's flat is *not* a proper holiday,' Will grouched, then immediately wished he could suck the words back. His grandfather might have been a loser who wanted nothing to do with them, but his mum was still struggling. It had been months since Rex Davenant died. No death was easy. And as Will knew far too well, some were almost impossible.

'Sorry,' he muttered. 'I'm just really hot.'

He felt Mary's hand on his knee.

'It's OK, kiddo,' she whispered. 'And if you think you've got problems, wait till I tell you about the wee I've needed since Winchester . . .'

Will smiled. His mum could always make him smile. Even on the days when Will had thought he'd never smile again.

'Let's take our minds off it. The number plate game!' Mary said brightly. 'That Hyundai over there, last three letters are HFM . . . Hairy Ferret Man.'

Will threw his head back on the headrest and closed his eyes.

'It's too hot,' he groaned. 'I can't think.'

A cold splash to his face made him gasp.

'Wakey-wakey, then,' his mum giggled with a wink, putting her water bottle to her lips. 'Huge Fairy Mullet? Happy Furry Martian? Howling Fish Moron? Hiccuping Flying Mouse?'

'Hopeless Forty Mother?' Will offered with a sly grin.

'Oi!' Mary cried, squirting him again. 'I'm not forty for

months! So start saving up for my present!'

Will tried to smile, but this time he couldn't. He'd love nothing more than to buy his mum a massive present for her fortieth, or throw her a great party, or take her to her favourite restaurant. Dad would have done all of that and more. They'd talked about surprising Mum with a trip to a hotel, or one of those fancy spas in magazines, or maybe taking the train to Paris. But none of those things would happen now. There would be no hotel. Will had no money for a spa. And there was more chance of the tooth fairy taking them to Paris than Uncle Claude.

Because that's what happened when Will lost his dad.

He'd lost all their dreams as well.

'Hey,' said his mum softly, reaching for his hand and reading his mind like she always seemed to. 'We'll have a great time whatever we do. Do you remember that breakfast in bed you made me for Mother's Day?'

'Yeah?' Will grimaced, recalling the burnt toast and concrete eggs.

'Well,' Mary whispered, 'don't do that again, kiddo, and I'll have a wonderful birthday.'

Will playfully slapped his mum's hand away.

'High Five Mum,' Mary cheered triumphantly. 'Although I still really need that wee . . .'

The car inched forward again, slightly faster this time, generating enough of a breeze to cool Will's thoughts.

Mum was right. A break would be good. The seaside was all right. And anywhere was better than Uncle Claude's.

His mum's brother had 'kindly' taken them in after Will's dad had died. Mary had tried to pay the rent and bills on her own. But the job she loved, helping people find emergency housing, ironically couldn't keep a roof over her own head. So they moved in with Claude. And he was determined to remind them how kind he'd been every day.

Uncle Claude had 'kindly' given Mary the box room he used for storage and 'kindly' let her cook and clean for him and his son Jon to repay his generosity.

Uncle Claude had 'kindly' agreed that Will could sleep on the sofa bed in the utility room, so long as Will was up every day at five-thirty a.m. with the bed tidied away so that Claude didn't have to be reminded of his warm-heartedness when he left for work at six. Not that Will ever got to sleep in that long.

Uncle Claude 'kindly' gave Mary a job as a secretary in his office, then kept nearly all of her wages to finance his goodness.

Will didn't know how he could ever repay Uncle Claude's 'kindness'. But he certainly knew he couldn't take much more of it.

'Beggars can't be choosers,' his uncle would snarl as Will wore Jon's threadbare hand-me-downs and ate lukewarm leftovers and watched his mother being treated like an unpaid servant just to make sure they had somewhere to live. Mary used to have fire in her eyes. But Uncle Claude had dimmed it to barely a flicker.

'It won't be forever,' his mum promised daily. Will hoped she was right. Because it had only been two years. But it already felt like an eternity.

'At last!' Mary exclaimed, wiping the sweat from her head as the traffic finally started to move. 'We're out of first gear! We're on our way! At least Uncle Claude got the gearbox fixed.'

But as their car made a Horribly Fractured Moan and spluttered to a slow, shuddering halt, it became clear that, once again, Uncle Claude had been his typically 'kind' self.

Three hours later, they finally arrived at Arden Heights after two miserable hours spent on the side of the motorway and a worse one in the Doug Berry Repairs tow truck. After sixty-two minutes with Doug, Will knew two things about their rescuer: one – he was very proud of his neighbourhood watch, and two – he really liked egg sandwiches. Will could have lived a long and happy life without either piece of information.

'At least he has air con,' Mary whispered as Will

struggled against the nasal assault of Doug's third sandwich.

'Yeah,' Will said, breathing in through his mouth. 'At least now we'll suffocate cold.'

'. . . and so I walked up to the fella, bold as grass, and comprehended him in broad nightlight,' Doug chortled. 'I was as proud as lunch! Oh – speaking o' which – you want some?'

He offered his half-eaten sandwich to his passengers. Will tried not to gag.

'We're good, thanks,' Mary grimaced politely, jiggling around in her seat. She still hadn't had her wee.

'Shame,' said Doug, chomping down on his butty again. 'I shouldn't have brung so many – I've got eyes bigger than me bum. Any road, did I tell you about the time I stopped her from number 38 from putting her bins out on the wrong night?'

'You didn't!' Mary said enthusiastically, winking at Will. 'But if it's half as good as the one about Mr Verge's leaf blower, we're in for a treat . . .'

By the time they reached the block of flats, the August sun had long since retired for the night. As Will burst out of the cab of the truck and took his first deep breath for over an hour, the evening air still felt sticky and close around his warm skin. He couldn't wait to take a long, cold shower and wash this horrible day away.

'You're kidding,' Mary said to Doug, who somehow still hadn't finished his egg sandwich. 'Someone's parked in our space!'

Will looked at the space designated for flat 29, which was occupied by a big blue people carrier.

'Well, I'll be,' said Doug disapprovingly. 'Reminds me of the time Debbie Quickly parked her Ford Cortina in front of Marie Fenton's driveway – they fought like cats and frogs, I tell you. Where d'ya wannit, my love?'

'Urgh,' sighed Mary, pulling her damp T-shirt away from her damper body. 'Just leave it in one of the visitors' spaces – you can pick it up from there in the morning.'

'I'll do it on the triple,' said Doug cheerfully, saluting them both. 'Your wish is my demand.'

'Thanks, Doug,' Mary said kindly. 'I don't know what we would have done without you.'

'Breathe properly?' Will muttered, to a stealthy poke from his mother.

'You're welcome, my sweet,' said the driver, pulling their suitcases out of the cab before clambering back into it. 'Always happy to lend a foot. Mind how you go now.'

Mary and Will each grabbed a case, along with the now-ruined food they had brought from London, and headed towards the entrance to Arden Heights. Will couldn't make much out in the gloom – it was much darker down here on the unlit coast than in the illuminated city – but what reared up ahead of him was a brown-brick block of flats with balconies dotted around the three sides of the square building, some of the residents sitting out in the warm evening air. As they walked around its perimeter to the front door, Will could just make out that the block was set in a pretty garden with a swimming pool at its heart. He looked longingly at the mass of water, desperate to jump in and feel its coolness against his skin . . .

But he couldn't.

Will was aware that Mary had come to a halt. He looked over at his mum, whose face was a strange mixture of feelings he couldn't pull apart.

'You see? Told you we'd have fun,' Mary said quietly. She tore her eyes away from the building and gestured to the pool. 'I can't remember the last time we went swimming.'

Will felt a familiar and uncomfortable sensation twist in his stomach. He could remember exactly when they'd last swum. It was on their final holiday with Dad before he got ill, not that they'd known it would be their final holiday then. They'd had no idea when they laughed and joked in that caravan in the Lake District, or splashed around in the sparkling lake, or played card games in front of their campfire, that their happy story was about to take the saddest twist. Will would have loved to swim in that pool with his mum. But there was no way that was going to happen this week.

'Now, I know it's on here somewhere,' said Mary with false brightness, pulling a bunch of keys out of her over-stuffed handbag. 'Or at least I think it is – I never took it off for some reason.'

Will watched Mary struggle with a thought that she quickly threw away. He wasn't entirely sure what had happened between his mum and her dad. He knew it had something to do with his own father, Leo. And he knew that Rex – Will only ever used his first name, Rex hadn't earned the title 'Grandad' – disapproved of his mum being with his dad, although he didn't really know why. Leo had only spoken of it once and Will could only remember a single piece of information.

'Your mother was forced to make a choice. And she chose us,' he had said proudly. 'So we must always choose her.'

It always amazed Will that he still had any tears left to cry over his dad – surely there couldn't be any more inside? But as he thought how his dad would have happily chosen his mum every day of his life, had he been allowed, he could feel a fresh crop rising to his tired eyes.

'Here we go!' Mary declared triumphantly, holding a

strange-shaped square key from her key ring. 'Right – let's get inside, get washed up and get some food down us.'

She peered into the plastic bags at the sweaty, soggy remains of the leftovers Uncle Claude had 'kindly' let them take from the fridge that morning.

'Takeaway it is,' she said with a grin. 'Uncle Claude gave me some money for his new bedroom curtains and I haggled the man down. So we've got twenty pounds he's not going to miss – we'll eat like kings! Now, let's get inside.'

'Oi!' came an aggressive shout from across the car park. Will lurched his tired head around. What now?

'This is private property!' yelled the older man hobbling towards them, threateningly waving a broom. 'Residents only! So clear off!'

Will heard Mary exhale next to him. His mum was very good at diffusing difficult situations – living with Uncle Claude had given her plenty of practice. She took a second deep breath and turned around with a forced smile.

'Good evening,' she said, extending her hand. 'I'm Mary. Nice to meet you. And you are?'

'Caleb,' the man growled, not taking Mary's hand, nor offering a surname. 'Arden Heights caretaker. What business have you here?'

'I'm Rex Davenant's daughter,' Mary said, her voice

hardening at Caleb's rudeness. 'I'm here to . . . I'm here to sort out his flat.'

The old man stopped and scrutinized them both. He put the broom down, although not his suspicious gaze.

'So the prodigal daughter has returned,' he said unpleasantly. 'The Duke told me all about you.'

'Who's the Duke?' Will whispered out of the corner of his mouth.

'Dad's nickname,' Mary whispered back. 'He loved jazz. Haven't heard him called that in years.'

'I've got a few other names for him,' Will muttered.

'And you must be the boy,' Caleb pronounced, nodding dismissively in Will's direction.

'Yes, this is my son, Will,' said Mary through a clenched jaw. Mary was always polite and reasonable with people. Right up to the point until she wasn't. And this Caleb was pushing his luck. 'Now we've had a long journey and are desperate for some food and some sleep, so if you'll excuse us . . .'

'You can't just dump your car there,' Caleb snarled. 'Them's for visitors.'

'Well, someone parked in our space,' Mary snapped. 'And we're just visiting. So that's all super, isn't it?'

Will had seen this before. Mum was brewing like a volcano before it erupted. Things were about to get molten.

'You need to move it!' Caleb barked. 'We have rules about this sort of thing! I'll be reporting you to the residents' committee and then there'll be all hell to pay, mark my—'

'I'll tell you what, Caleb,' Mary said firmly and rather loudly, moving menacingly towards the caretaker, who took a step backwards. 'I've had a very challenging day. My journey was long, my car is broken, my son and I are tired and hungry and I'm about to wet my pants. I'm not sure what you want me to do with a vehicle that has already failed to get us here once today, but if you want some suggestions, I've got a long and creative list of precisely WHERE I'D LIKE TO PUT IT!'

Will had to stifle a laugh as the elderly caretaker cowered slightly. Dad always described Mary as a 'firework'. It was good to see his mum's fire back. Uncle Claude hadn't managed to extinguish it entirely.

'Like I say,' Caleb growled. 'I'll be reporting you to the residents' committee.'

'Knock yourself out, Caleb!' said Mary brightly. 'Because there's a chicken chow mein with my name on it and nothing and no one is going to keep it from me! Right after I've had a MASSIVE WEE!'

And with an aggressive flourish, Mary turned the key in the door, her back on Caleb and ushered Will inside Arden Heights.

The heavy wooden door slammed behind them like a rude word.

'Well, he's a charmer,' Mary smiled at her son, calm restored to her face. 'C'mon, kiddo – let's get you to flat 29.'

They walked along the narrow hallway and turned right at the end towards a small lift. Ahead was a room with several tables covered in half-finished jigsaw puzzles and board games, a pool table and a dartboard.

'The rec – recreation – room,' Mary explained as she hit the button and stretched her tired neck. 'Most of the residents here are elderly, you see.'

Will was struck by the smell of the flats – it wasn't bad, it was just . . . different. He looked to where a bowl of very old potpourri had been placed on a glass table under an old mirror. His mum followed the direction of his gaze and laughed.

'I believe it was your grandmother who put that there,' she chuckled. 'The guy who lived at flat 2 used to smoke cigars – my mum was making a point. Classic Violet.'

Will did the maths. He knew his grandmother Violet had died when he was two, so that was eleven years ago. From what Will had gathered about his grandparents, they agreed on most things, but they certainly did not agree on Rex's treatment of his daughter. Grandma Violet had defied his order not to have anything to do with Mary and her new family, and Will knew that his mum missed her own very much.

But surely no one was going to miss potpourri that was at least eleven years old?

The lift pinged and Will and Mary slumped into it. There were four floors at Arden Heights – Mary hit the button for the second. Will looked at his mum. Until now, Mary had seemed quite relaxed. But as the lift neared its destination, he could smell the anxiety on her like Doug's egg sandwiches.

'You OK?' he asked her.

His mum looked confused, as if she wasn't entirely aware how she felt, nor that she was broadcasting it to her son.

'I'm fine,' she said with a reassuring smile. 'It's just . . . strange. I've not been here in forever.'

As the lift came to a halt, Will smiled back. His mum had already had to deal with far too much strangeness in the recent past. He hoped that this would be the last bit.

'Two pieces of good news,' Mary said as they approached the door to flat 29 and she put in another key. 'One – I now officially hold the world record for holding in a wee. And two – my father was a neat and tidy man. This really shouldn't take us that long—'

But as the door to her father's flat swung open, Mary stopped in her tracks.

'Oh,' was all she said.

Will peered around his mother to see what had silenced her so suddenly. The answer came back quickly.

His grandfather might have been a neat and tidy man. But his flat was an absolute tip.

CHAPTER II

Much Ado About Something

Rather like the day before it, Will's first night at Arden Heights didn't go entirely as planned. Having dreamt of a cold shower – and with Doug's sandwich still festering in his nostrils – Will discovered that flat 29 only had a bath. The choice between shivering in cold water or sweating in warm was not one Will relished – so he opted for a cold flannel around his hot skin. The takeaway was very welcome – even if he could have eaten twice as much – and by the time he slumped into bed, he hadn't really had time to look around.

But as the new day dawned – or at least when Will joined it at eleven a.m. – he awoke with a renewed curiosity about the unknown home of his unknown grandfather.

Flat 29 had two bedrooms – Mum was in Rex's double bedroom and Will was in the small spare room opposite, although judging by the amount of junk littered around, it hadn't entertained guests for some time. The previous night, he'd seen a living room, a small kitchen and a room that must have been Rex's office – it was the epicentre of the earthquake of papers that covered every surface. As Will dragged himself from the comfy single bed, he could hear his mum already moving around the flat. First impressions of Rex's home hadn't been great – but as he pulled his door open, many things looked better in the light of day.

Firstly, the flat wasn't exactly messy – it was just . . . busy. Piles of papers covered every surface – the hallway, the many bookshelves, even the bathroom was full of neatly bundled packages of documents. Will took a peek at the one nearest his bedroom door – it had a scribbled note on top of it that read: *1980–1981*. As he surveyed the nearby bundles, he could see they were all dated – there was at least some order to the chaos. A thought for a picture crossed his mind and he ran back to grab his pad, sketching a rough image of these bundles of papers creating a maze of skyscraper years for him to navigate. He looked satisfactorily on his draft. He'd come back and finish that later.

After a hot night that only sheer exhaustion had

helped him sleep through, Will's mouth was as dry as the beach below, so he headed to the compact kitchen next to his bedroom for a glass of water. But before he could reach it, he was stopped in his tracks by the view from the living room window.

It was the sea. A glorious, beautiful, uninterrupted view of the sea, sunlight leaping from the deep blue waves, stretching out into the unknown forever. Will had always lived in towns and never really understood why people got so excited about the ocean. But as he moved hypnotically towards the view, he finally got it.

'Pretty awesome, isn't it?' Mary whispered in his ear.

'It's . . . it's . . . wow,' Will spluttered as his mum opened the huge French windows so they could step on to the moss-covered balcony. As he tentatively gripped the white iron railings, the warm sea breeze stroked his skin and Will took his first breath of fresh, clean air. He'd never had a problem living in a big city. But here the very atmosphere felt nourishing and safe – cleaner somehow. He tilted his head, let the sun heat his face and looked out over the great blue beyond.

'So, you grew up here?' he asked his mum as she put her arm around his waist.

'No,' she replied, leaning forward on to the railings. 'This was my parents' holiday place. Dad moved here after Mum died. But we came every holiday. Being the child of two university professors wasn't always great in term-time – but the summers were awesome . . .'

Mary's thoughts drifted somewhere Will couldn't follow. Something about Mum had changed here already. She was . . . lighter. Stronger. She took up more space – in a good way. And her face . . . maybe it was the sunlight illuminating it? Or maybe it was the face itself.

'Right,' she said, pushing herself off the railings. 'Kiddo, we have a job to do. I'm working my way through my father's study – which is going to take most of the rest of my life, FYI – can you start packing up his books? I've left some boxes in his bedroom. Most of it can go to the charity shop, but if you see anything worth keeping, put it to one side. There are quite a few . . .'

Will looked around the book-lined walls of every square centimetre of the flat. Yes. There were quite a few. A resentful thought spilt into his mind – why were he and his mum having to do this anyway? Rex hadn't wanted anything to do with them, why should they clean up his mess? But it was Jon's nineteenth birthday that weekend and Uncle Claude had told them he didn't want them around, so off they'd gone. Will trudged reluctantly from the balcony, walked through to the kitchen to grab a bowl of cereal and then on to his grandfather's bedroom.

Rather like the potpourri downstairs, Will suspected

that the room hadn't been changed in many years. Facing the same way as the living room, the bedroom enjoyed the same incredible sea view – Will could only imagine how amazing it would be waking up to that vista every morning. Or indeed, waking up to anything but his uncle, cousin and the tumble dryer. The bedroom itself was cosy, if a bit old-fashioned. The floral wallpaper didn't entirely match with the also floral curtains and the unnecessarily floral bedspread. But Will could sense his grandmother's touch here. And he figured that might be why Rex hadn't changed it.

He grabbed a cardboard box and crouched down in front of the tall bookshelf in Rex's bedroom. All of the books felt old, looked expensive and smelt of intelligence. There were dictionaries, encyclopaedias, poetry collections, novels by writers that Will had heard of and many by ones he had not. A weird pang of guilt that he hadn't inherited his grandfather's, nor his mother's love of books, twitched in his chest. He liked stories. But he didn't really enjoy reading.

'We just do better with stories we can see,' his dad had explained, sharing Will's love of graphic novels and movies. 'Stories are like fruit – doesn't matter how you consume them, so long as you take plenty on board. Some folk tell stories with words; you tell yours with pictures.'

Leo had been a brilliant artist. Will hoped that one

day he'd be even half as good. If his dad's family had been richer, Leo would have gone to art college – maybe been a famous artist. But he didn't and Will wouldn't. It wasn't fair. Why should only wealthy people afford to stay talented?

Shaking the thought from his head, Will packed each heavy book into the boxes. It wasn't a careful job – not his books, not his problem – but it did what was needed. He was just leaving to find something to clean the dusty shelves, when a final book caught his eye.

This one wasn't on a shelf – it was next to his grandfather's bed, almost hidden by the globe that sat next to it. He walked over, picked it up and was about to toss it in the box with the others when a strange sensation stirred inside him. It took him a moment to place it, it had been so long since he had experienced it. But it was there. And after a while, he recognized it.

It was curiosity.

He sat on the side of the bed. All of Rex's books were old, but this one was positively ancient. It had been face down on the bedside table, so Will had to carefully turn it in his hands to see the title on the front cover. Was it a book of magic? Of spells? Of curses?

But as Will made out the faded gold lettering, his heart sank at the words that formed before his disappointed eyes:

Now *this* writer, Will knew something about. He'd been forced to study one of Shakespeare's plays in Year Seven – something about fairies and people running around a wood looking like a donkey. He hadn't got it. The words were weird and he didn't understand the story. One play had been more than enough – but here was a whole massive book of them. His curiosity dissolved, Will was about to drop it in the box, when something fluttered out from between the pages. It was a photograph of a boy. A boy who looked just like him.

He held the black-and-white photograph up to the light. Upon closer inspection, it wasn't him – he wouldn't be seen dead in those old clothes – but, wow, did he and this kid look alike. The boy in the picture smiled at him mischievously. And he was holding this same book, the Shakespeare one. Will turned the photograph over. There was a handwritten inscription scrawled on the back:

The Bard
June 1954

Will was intrigued. This photo was taken decades before he was born. And yet . . . He'd never seen a photo of Rex – why would he want to? But if this was him, they looked like twins. There was the curiosity again – who was this man, with whom he shared some genetics, but no part of his life? Perhaps there would be more clues inside the book? Will had zero interest in the plays – weird words, no story – but what was this photograph doing inside it?

He carefully placed the book on the floor. It was as thick as a shoebox and slightly wider. Will wiped some of the dust from the cover with his palms, before rubbing it off on his jeans – his mum would wash them, it would be fine. The golden lettering that spelt the playwright's name glistened more brightly for the cleaning, the sunlight bouncing off the ocean beyond and illuminating the famous name that had shone through the generations. Conventional wisdom said that you should never judge a book by its cover, but in this case, it was the other way around. He knew what was inside – he could still remember his Year Seven English teacher Mr Pinch talking about someone called Bottom – but the cover of this book was beautiful. It was plain – brown leather with nothing but the gold lettering on the front. There was just . . . something about it. Something that marked it out as special. Will had no particular interest in books. This one, though . . .

The book was already thick – Shakespeare used loads of words, Will recalled. But he could also see that the many pages were stuffed with other things. The photograph that had just fallen out, but also other pieces of paper that didn't look as though they belonged to the original book – letters, notes, newspaper clippings – what were they doing there?

Will reached for the bottom right corner to raise the thick cover. It was worn in places, but still intact, and holding the pages firmly in its grasp, he curled his fingertips under the corner of the cover and started to lift it.

The moment his skin made contact with the book, a glow – or what his tired eyes thought was a glow – seeped from the pages. Will blinked heavily. It had been a tiring couple of days and he didn't entirely trust his own brain. But his mind and eyesight agreed – the book was lighting up from the inside, as though someone had lit a lantern within it.

Half-terrified, half-fascinated, Will tightened his pinch on the corner of the book. Some deep impulse urged him to open the cover, to reveal whatever secret was hidden within. He knew that he shouldn't. But he also knew that he would. So with a deep breath and a bold heart, he grasped on to the cover and—

'Will!' his mum yelled from the study across the hallway. 'Are you done yet? I could use a hand in here!'

Will snatched his fingers away like they had been burnt. He hadn't done anything wrong and yet he felt as guilty as if Doug had caught him on his neighbourhood watch. He looked back at the book, which had returned to its usual colour. Or had it been that way all along? Will reached out again—

'WILL!' came Mary's insistent voice. 'I need those muscles, you great lug!'

'Coming!' Will cried before his brain knew what his mouth had done. He picked up the book and went to put it on the pile with all the others. But some deep, insistent impulse stopped him. He hugged the book to him, crossed the hallway and hastily deposited it on his bedroom floor. He looked at it once more. Was he losing his mind?

He'd just saved Shakespeare from the charity shop.

Yup. Something was definitely weird.

Will left his bedroom, shutting the door behind him – something instinctively told him this book needed to be protected. Rex's office was diagonally opposite and at first he couldn't see his mum for the piles of boxes between him and her.

'We need more space,' said Mum, popping up like a whack-a-mole in the middle of a city of boxes and papers. 'Grab *1994–2006* and take them into the hallway, it's chaos in here. I think Dad was trying to write his memoirs – and he kept copies of absolutely everything he ever wrote, saw or bought. This is going to take all week.'

Will stifled a groan as he felt his summer holiday slipping away. His mum had promised him a week by the seaside. But this was shaping up to be just like Uncle Claude's house – a lot of work and no reward. With a heavy sigh, he picked up two document boxes marked *1997* and *2003* and dropped them outside the flat, before returning for *1999* and *2001.* He was about to come back straining under *1994/5* and *6* when he was interrupted by a crash, a shout and a word that Mum had made clear he wasn't allowed to use until he was at least fifty.

'WHAT THE ABSOLUTE **** **** IS ANYONE DOING LEAVING ALL THESE **** BOXES IN THE **** WAY?!!!!' the man yelled, for it was a man Will could see hopping around in the hallway. Will wasn't sure what to do – should he apologize? Should he retreat to the flat? Should he call his mum?

But as the man turned around and aimed his furious gaze at Will, it quickly became clear that the one thing he probably shouldn't have done was stand there with his arms full of boxes.

'WHAT— What do you think you're doing?!' the man shouted from the middle of the pile of papers his fall had spread all over the hallway.

'I . . . er . . . I'm really . . . I was just . . .' Will burbled as the man nursed his foot. He was probably about his mum's age – so quite old – and despite the summer heat, was wearing a suit, the collar open at the neck and his tie undone against the ferocious temperature.

'I'll ask you again!' the man challenged. 'What were you thinking? I could have broken my neck!'

'Well, it still appears to be yapping, so I'm guessing you'll live,' came the firm tones of a woman prepared to be reasonable until she wasn't. 'May I help you?'

'You may,' the man snapped, picking up his papers, 'by not leaving your rubbish out in the hallway for people to trip over!'

'A person's life story is not rubbish,' Mary said pointedly. 'And if *people* spent less time with their heads up their own backsides and more time watching where they were going, perhaps they'd not trip over? The boxes will be gone by the end of the day. But *you* should please feel free to leave sooner.'

Will stood in between these two adults, awkwardly holding his boxes. Surely that would be an end to it? This man must see there was no point in arguing with Mary when she was—

'If you put half as much energy into tidying as you do into talking, you'll be finished by lunchtime,' the man declared.

Will closed his eyes and sighed. He loved his mum. But she could be a spectacular last-word freak. This guy had no idea what he'd let himself in for.

'And why would I do that?' his mum replied with fake sweetness. 'When you've so kindly offered to break your neck.'

'Better than listening to you,' the man muttered as Will finally put his boxes down and went to help pick up the fallen papers. He turned the first of the identical pages over and read it:

Save Arden Heights!

Vote AGAINST on Friday!

YOUR COMMUNITY NEEDS YOU!

'Give me that,' said the man, snatching the paper from Will's hand. 'And believe me when I say I will be making a complaint to whatever cleaning firm you work for.'

'Cleaning firm!' Mary cried. 'I'm Mary Davenant. Rex's daughter.'

This stopped the man in his tracks. Will watched him wince as he realized why they were leaving the boxes out in the hall.

'I'm so sorry,' he said quietly. 'For your loss, I mean. I've not been here long, but I met Rex a few times. He was a true gentleman.'

Will watched his mum nod back. And noted that she

looked deeply smug.

'I didn't know Rex had a daughter,' the man continued. 'He never said . . .'

Mary's jaw twitched.

'No,' she said simply. 'I don't suppose he did.'

'Well, then,' said their visitor, attempting a more friendly tone. 'You might be able to help us. Arden Heights is under threat from a developer called Egeus. We need just twenty flats to object to the proposal and then we can—'

'Save your breath,' said Mary, holding up a hand to stop the hail of words coming her way. 'It's nothing to do with me. My brother owns this flat.'

'Right,' the man stuttered. 'Claude, isn't it?'

'Oh, good,' muttered Mary. 'Rex talked about his son, then. But you'll have to take it up with him. I'm just here to clear up. Like I say, it isn't my flat.'

'They won't be anyone's flats, if Egeus has its way,' she was sharply told. 'But clearly you don't care about other people, so I'll save my breath.'

Will had several questions. But he wasn't getting a word in with a crowbar.

'Is it National Idiot Day?' Mary shot back. 'I must have missed it.'

'Such a shame,' her new enemy quipped, 'when it was arranged in your honour.'

'Congratulations,' Mary said with a slow handclap. 'You're officially the most obnoxious person in this building.'

'Gracious of you to concede the title,' the man said with a bow.

Will braced himself for the tirade he knew was about to erupt from his mother's mouth – although it was good to see more fire back in her eyes. But he – and this poor fool – were spared from it by the door to flat 30 opening next to them.

'Ah, Ben, how lovely to see you,' said a smiling grey-haired lady with a sugary lilt to her words. 'How are you and your little one getting along? The first few months of a move can be so overwhelming.'

'Er . . . well, thank you, Angela,' Ben replied, rather more politely than he'd spoken to Mary. 'And thank you so much for the lasagne, it was a very kind thought. Again. Please don't feel you need to keep—'

'Pah – it was nothing,' Angela said with a dismissive wave. 'And it won't be a patch on what you're used to. You live with such a wonderful cook.'

'I can lend your wife some arsenic if she needs it?' Mary said brightly. 'Just tell her to pop round, it would be my neighbourly pleasure.'

Ben turned to Mary with a hard stare.

'Angela was referring to my mother,' he said coldly.

'And she won't be cooking anything as she's seriously unwell – which is why we've moved down here to care for her.'

Will watched his mother shift uncomfortably.

'I'm so sorry,' she said sincerely. 'For your mother, I mean. I hope she recovers soon.'

Ben nodded, looking more than a little smug himself, Will noted.

'And you must be Mary,' said Angela warmly, coming forward to greet Will's mum. 'Claude told me you'd be coming down – isn't he a charming chap? It must be lovely to have a big brother to take care of you.'

Mary's lips pursed tightly.

'Words can't express it,' she said eventually.

'That'll make a pleasant change,' Ben muttered, earning him a death stare from his new neighbour.

'My dear,' said Angela earnestly, moving forward to take Mary's hands in hers. 'I am so, so sorry for your father's passing. Rex was a much-loved member of our community at Arden Heights – and a wonderful head of our residents' committee. He will be sorely missed.'

Will felt a surge of irritation as he wanted to tell this woman precisely what his grandfather and uncle were really like. But he said nothing. He never did.

'And welcome to Arden Heights, young man,' Angela said to Will. 'It's always lovely to have young blood around the place – I'm afraid we're a lot of old fuddy-duddies here, I'm sure you'll liven it up. Although not too loudly, I hope. Now what's your favourite meal? I'm sure your mum's not had a minute to cook. Let me make you something for your supper.'

'Oh, Angela, that's very kind, but we're—' Mary began.

'I like lasagne too,' Will interrupted. His mum was very bad at accepting help. And he was really good at eating pasta.

'Then it's a done deal – I'll hear no more about it,' Angela insisted with a smile. 'I'll drop it around before the election tonight.'

'Ah, yes. How's your campaign going?' Ben asked. 'I got your letter. And the biscuits. And the wine.'

'It was my absolute pleasure!' Angela trilled. 'But Julian is a wonderful candidate too, I'll be happy to lose to him.'

'Candidate?' Mary enquired politely.

'Oh, it's a nonsense really,' Angela blustered. 'Your sainted father's passing left a gaping hole at the helm of the residents' committee, we haven't had the heart to fill it. But with the Egeus vote coming up someone needs to run the show. Myself and my good friend Julian from flat 20 have thrown our hats into the ring. The election is tonight.'

'Well, good luck,' said Mary. 'Now if you'll excuse me, we've got rather a lot to do . . .'

'Oh, listen to me chattering on,' giggled Angela. 'I'll be back later with that lasagne – and I'm sure I can rustle up some chocolate cake for pudding too, young Phil!'

'Erm, actually, it's . . .' Mary started to explain. But Angela was already drawing her next breath.

'I'm right here next door if you need anything – anything at all, just ask Angela!'

She smiled at Will and pinched his cheek. He didn't really like it. But he was prepared to trade it off for a chocolate cake. Angela walked back into her flat, Ben nodding a curt farewell as he walked towards the lift.

'Oh, one last thing, Ben,' said Angela as he entered the lift. 'Would you mind moving that lovely big car of yours. You're parked in Mary's space.'

'WHAT?!' Mary screamed, as the doors closed on Ben's smiling face.

CHAPTER III

The Tempest

After several tedious hours of wading through Rex's papers, Mary turned to Will with a tired sigh.

'Right, kiddo, get outside and get some fresh air,' she declared. 'This is no place for a growing lad. Follow the path out of the back of the garden, it'll lead you straight down the steps to the beach. Be back for dinner.'

Will wanted to argue with his mum, to tell her he'd rather stay and help.

But he really didn't want to.

'OK,' he agreed, pulling himself up from his tired knees. 'If you insist.'

'Don't forget sun cream!' Mary shouted after him. 'Your T-shirts and shorts are in my case and it's hot out there!'

'Gotcha,' Will called back. He wouldn't need sun cream. He wasn't going to change out of his jumper and jeans. And there was no point in having that conversation with his mother.

He took the lift down to the ground floor and left the building, emerging into the warm sea air that embraced Arden Heights. Following his mother's instructions, he walked through the gardens, where four residents, two men and two women, were tending to the kaleidoscope of colourful plants that filled the pretty lawn.

'I'm telling you,' a woman in red overalls was insisting, 'if we deadhead the dahlias now, they'll bloom long into the autumn.'

'We need to be sowing our hardy annuals!' the other huffed, pulling a light blue headscarf back from her hot face.

'*You're* a hardy annual,' the first woman muttered.

'Come on now,' a man gently suggested, pulling a shovel from the belt around his green shorts. 'There's time to do both things.'

'You're not wrong,' the other amiably agreed in his salmon-pink trousers. 'Why don't we all—'

The first woman grabbed a pair of scissors and started aggressively cutting the heads off some flowers, much to the other woman's irritation. The two men shrugged at one another.

Will walked past the group with a smile. There was drama amongst the dahlias.

He found a small gateway in the hedgerow that opened on to a long, winding set of stone steps that, as his mum had told him, led straight down to the beach. The ocean looked every bit as inviting as it had from the flat. Will walked across the promenade and stood on the edge of the beach with a sad smile. He hadn't been to the seaside since before his dad had died. As a family, they'd never had much money, but his dad always made everything fun. One year they'd seen donkey rides on the beach. His dad told him there was no need to pay silly money for one when they had their very own donkey here – Leo then spent the next hour cantering around making donkey noises with his son on his back. Will had laughed until his stomach hurt – and they'd spent the money they'd saved on a Mr Whippy. Will wished he'd known how happy he was back then. It shouldn't have taken the darkness for him to appreciate the light.

His feet meandered down to the shore where Will removed his shoes and socks – it was so hot in his jumper. The sand felt warm and soft between his toes and with every step, he felt body and mind relax. The day had been hard, but life felt easier here. He hated his school and he hated his home. If the years since his father died had been a bad dream, he needed to wake up quickly.

The sand grew damp beneath his feet. He imagined himself slowly turning into a fish the closer he got to the water, the call of the sea releasing him from his shackles on land and giving him the freedom of the ocean. He locked the visual in his mind to sketch it later. What he wouldn't give to run into the cool waves – surely no one would see him here? The crowds of tourists were packing up and leaving and it seemed unlikely anyone from Arden Heights would know or recognize him. Could he risk it?

But before the thought had half-formed in his mind, he felt the choice being ripped away by a shape in the sea catching his eye. At first he wasn't sure if what he was seeing was really there – it had been a busy couple of days and he knew he was tired.

As he focused hard on the lapping water, however, it became clear that his first thought was the correct one.

There was a boy floating face down in the water.

Had Will stopped to think, there were many better alternatives to the one he chose. This was a busy tourist beach, there would surely be a lifeguard nearby? Perhaps he could have alerted some of the departing beachgoers to help him? Even just shouting for assistance would have made more sense.

But Will Davenant simply ran straight into the sea.

He hadn't been in the water for a while – and a jumper

and jeans did not make it easy to wade through the waves. But he wasn't going to stand back and watch this boy drown. When the water reached his waist, he was forced to stop walking and start swimming. Now the weight of his clothing really started to impede him, his woollen jumper drinking all the nearby ocean, determined to drag him down. But Will was determined too – and the boy was only a few strokes out of his grasp.

The stricken child was face down, arms and legs outstretched – his left arm was Will's nearest point of contact, so he grabbed it and began the return journey to shore. As Will moved them both towards the beach, the boy started to struggle – that meant that he was breathing at least. But it was making an already challenging swim even harder. Will paddled resolutely for land, despite the spluttered protests and flailing that were coming from the body now attached to his. The moment he was back in his depth, he stood up, pulled the victim to his feet and awaited the grateful thanks that were surely coming his way.

Three things immediately became clear.

Firstly, he wasn't a boy. She was a girl.

Secondly, she wasn't drowning. But she was absolutely furious.

So thirdly, he wasn't getting any grateful thanks any time soon.

'WHAT DO YOU THINK YOU'RE DOING?!' screamed the not-boy in front of him.

'I thought I was saving your life?' Will said simply.

'Well, I think you're a moron!' she fired back. 'I was on the cusp of achieving a personal best for holding my breath under water until you blundered in!'

Will wasn't entirely sure how to respond to this unexpected attack.

'You're welcome,' he said eventually.

'Urgh!' the girl huffed, trudging out of the water and pushing her short black hair away from her face. Will waded out after her, his sodden clothes weighing heavily.

The girl picked up the towel slung over the bag that Will had failed to notice and aggressively towelled her hair, which spiked out around her face like petals on a sunflower as it dried. A phone was pulled out of her bag, a selfie was taken and it was posted to something.

'On behalf of the whole world, thanks for letting us know you dried your hair,' Will muttered. He didn't get social media. It was so . . . pointless.

'Just giving my followers what they want,' she said, posing for another picture.

Will snatched a look over the top of her phone.

'What, all seven?' he laughed. 'Although if that's what you post, I can see why.'

'It's quality, not quantity,' she snapped, tossing the phone back in her bag. 'And my mum likes to see what I'm doing – she's a singer, she's always travelling— Urgh, you're dripping everywhere – here.'

She tossed the damp towel his way.

'Gee, thanks,' he said, dabbing at his wet clothes. 'So great to meet you. Promise I won't ever try to save your life again.'

Will smiled sarcastically and started trudging back across the sand towards Arden Heights and some dry clothes. He pulled his heavy legs across the sand, the granules clinging to every atom of his wet body. How was he going to explain this to Mum?

'Oh, for— Wait!' came the shout behind him as he heard swift footsteps run towards him. 'Look, I'm sorry. You were trying to do a good thing. If I had been in trouble I'd have been lucky to have you there. Thank you.'

She stuck out her right hand, which Will cautiously accepted.

'Ani,' she said with a smile. 'A-N-I. Nice to sort of meet you.'

'Will,' Will replied cautiously. 'W-I-L-L. Nice to sort of be met.'

Ani pumped his arm enthusiastically.

'I'd better get home. I'm staying with a family friend while my mum's on tour, he'll be doing his nut,' she explained. 'But thanks for not saving my life.'

Will smiled.

'Anytime,' he replied. 'I'd better get back too. I have lasagne and a chocolate cake not to save.'

'Ha!' Ani said. 'That's weird, that was my dinner last night. Anyway, good to meet you.'

They went their separate ways. Although it turned out after a few awkward moments walking alongside each other, that their ways weren't that separate at all.

'Er . . . why are you following me?' Ani asked as they reached the bottom of the steps back to the flat. 'I told you, I'm fine.'

'Um, I know,' Will said slowly. 'The place I'm staying is up here.'

'But this only leads to Arden Heights,' Ani replied.

'And that's where I'm going,' Will confirmed.

Ani stopped, took a step back and eyed Will suspiciously.

'Wait,' she said. 'I've never seen you there. And I'd know if I had – there's hardly anyone there under seventy.'

'I only got here last night,' Will insisted, taking the first step to claim ownership. 'My grandfather has – had – a flat there.'

Ani strode over and took the first two steps, giving her a small height advantage.

'How convenient,' she said. 'Who is – was – your grandfather?'

Will took the next two steps to reply to her.

'He was called Mr Business,' he said. 'First names: None of Your.'

'Is he Team For or Team Against?' Ani asked suspiciously ascending three. 'Because Team For are going to destroy this community and everyone who loves this place and—'

'Do you have sea water on the brain or something?' Will answered, reclaiming the advantage.

'Cute,' said Ani, skipping up the next four steps. 'But how do I know you're not a weirdo?'

'You don't,' shrugged Will, jumping up the next five. 'But I already know you're one.'

'Am not!' Ani cried, shoving past him.

'Says the girl who plays dead in the sea,' puffed Will in what was now an all-out race to the top of the stairs.

The climb up the steep, uneven steps took any further smart remark Will had left out of his body – he needed all of his breath just to make it to the top, not that Ani seemed to be struggling like he was. They both took the steps two, three at a time until Arden Heights reared up before them. Ani and Will reached the top at precisely the same moment, still no clearer on who had won.

'Look, just leave me alone!' Ani said at the top of the

steps. 'I don't want you following–'

'Anishka Hathaway!' a familiar male voice boomed across the gardens. 'Where on earth have you been? I've been worried!'

'Oh, great,' Ani gulped as the man strode towards them. 'Ben, chill.'

Will recognized the figure looming before him. And it soon appeared that the man recognized him too.

'You again?' Ben said accusingly. 'Ani, is this boy bothering you?'

Ani looked at Will and he waited for her to land him straight in it.

'No,' she sighed. 'He's just some kid I met on the beach.'

She gave him a look that said: *Do NOT tell him how we met.* Will decided to heed it.

'Well, you need to come upstairs. I need to get Mum fed and washed before the election and we'll–'

'You again! I thought I told you to leave us alone!' came another familiar voice. 'Will, is this man harassing you? Why are you soaking wet?'

Will looked at his mother charging across the gardens towards them.

'Mum, it's fine,' he said soothingly before nodding towards Ani. 'She's just some kid I met on the beach.'

Ani shot him a dirty look, before turning to Ben.

'Er, hold on – how do you all know each other?' she asked.

'Oh, we had the pleasure earlier,' Mary hissed. 'We're staying here this week.'

'Told you,' Will grumbled at Ani, who merely rolled her eyes.

'You need to get a shift on,' Mary instructed Will. 'Angela has left enough food to feed a small army and the least we can do is go and vote for her at this election tonight. Doug is here to pick up the car – he brought sandwiches – so go upstairs and dry off and I'll see you in a mo.'

Will walked back towards the flats with his two new acquaintances, the awkward silence between him, Ani and Ben growing even more awkward as they walked into the building and were forced into the lift together.

'Floor?' Ani asked.

'Erm, two, please,' Will replied, feeling very small beside the very large Ben next to him.

'Oh, wow – us too!' Ani chirped. 'Which flat?'

'Ani,' Ben said in a warning tone, but she just rolled her eyes at him.

'29,' Will replied.

'We're 23!' she said. 'We're neighbours! How weird is that?'

'Very,' said Will, catching Ben's hard stare and

wishing he hadn't.

It was an excruciating ascent to the second floor, where Will gratefully spilt out of the lift doors. But standing in his way was an elderly lady, with long white hair flowing down to the waist of her dressing gown. She looked lost and confused, although she clearly wasn't a stranger to Ben and Ani.

'Olivia Touchstone!' Ani cried, taking the frail elderly woman's arm. 'What are you doing out here? Let's get you back to the flat.'

But Olivia wasn't moving. She simply stared at Will.

'Rex,' she said softly, reaching a hand towards Will with a happy smile. 'I knew you'd come. I knew you'd come back to me.'

'No, Mum,' Ben said gently, trying to steer his mother away. 'Rex isn't here, he's—'

'Did you tell her?' Olivia asked earnestly, grabbing Will's hands. 'Because I have it. I've kept it safe, I promise.'

Will didn't understand what Olivia was talking about. But there was something so . . . honest about the way she spoke to him. Like she knew something. Something he needed to hear. She leant in closer to him.

'They need you,' Olivia whispered to Will. 'Open the book. Tell your story. Set them free.'

'Come on, Liv. Let's get you home,' Ani said, guiding

the frail woman down the corridor. Ben watched for a moment before turning to Will.

'I'm sorry,' he said stiffly. 'Mum's rather confused these days. I hope she didn't upset you.'

'It's fine,' said Will. 'I didn't even know Rex, so . . .'

Ben nodded and briefly looked as though he wanted to say something else. But he did not, electing instead to head down the corridor after his mother and Ani and into flat 23.

But Will's mind was still buzzing with Olivia's words.

Open the book.

And somehow, he knew precisely which book she meant.

CHAPTER IV

All the World's a Page

Will rushed into flat 29, which was already filled with the heavy scent of Angela's lasagne. Normally, nothing could keep Will Davenant from a hearty meal, he didn't see nearly enough of them. But even with his damp clothes chafing his skin, Olivia's mysterious words were burning in his mind.

He went into his bedroom, locked the door in case his mum suddenly returned, and picked up the *Complete Works*, which he had left there earlier that day. He placed it carefully on the bed before kneeling next to it. The sheer insanity of what he was doing floated briefly across his mind. It had not been the easiest couple of years – was he actually losing it? Possibly. But this book had a story. And Will was determined to hear it.

He stared down at the book again. It was so old – the

original pages were browning and many of the documents peeking out from within its pages looked as though they might disintegrate at the slightest touch. Before he had really thought about what he was doing, he reached towards the leather cover again. His fingertips hovered over it. Was this a good idea? Dad had always counselled, 'Don't trouble trouble, if trouble isn't troubling you.' But Will's brain overrode his caution. It was just a book, what was the worst that could happen? And if he were honest with himself, the chances were that absolutely nothing was going to happen anyway. Olivia was very unwell, Rex hadn't perhaps been his best self when he put this book away, and now he thought about it, this was all a bit stupid.

But he still needed to know for sure.

Closing his eyes and screwing his courage . . . somewhere, Will flipped the front cover open with his forefinger. The moment it made contact with the duvet, he instinctively leapt backwards, making sure he kept a safe distance from—

Absolutely nothing at all.

A few cautious moments passed before Will allowed himself a small laugh at his own daftness. Of course nothing had happened, it was just a book. Just an old, boring book like the hundreds of others around his grandad's flat. Shaking his head, he crawled back across the floor to close it – the sooner all this was down the charity shop, the better. Now he could just have a wash, put on some dry clothes and—

And then it happened.

The moment Will touched the browning pages, the room was filled with shards of golden light. The sun was still burning the August evening outside – but these glowing rays weren't coming from outside the window. They were coming from inside the book. And they weren't beams of light, they were shapes – letters, he realized, as they lifted from the pages to form whole words in the air, his room filling with whispered sentences as they floated in the evening shimmer.

Will was both rooted to the spot and wanting to run screaming from the room, but as the golden letters evaporated in his bedroom, his eyes were drawn back to the open book. The swirl of words was most intense around the open pages, but rather than dissolve as the others had, they formed shapes on top of the book. They were trees and flowers and . . . bodies, three of them. A fourth, smaller shape started to emerge – was that a head? A whole scene was coming to life, like something out of a pop-up book, but these shapes weren't made from paper. They were flesh and bone and wood and petal. His room was filled with the scent of fresh woodland. And in the centre of this forest tableau, four characters appeared, like tiny actors on a stage: a middle-aged woman in a dark red robe, a teenage girl in a pink dress, a . . . fairy thing covered in leaves – and a skull. The smallest figure was no bigger than a clementine, the tallest the height of a pepper mill. Will didn't know whether to be terrified, to scream for help or to check into the nearest hospital. But as his grandfather's *Complete Works* came to life in front of him, Will knew he wasn't going anywhere.

These new creations also seemed to be a little confused and for a moment stood looking around Will's room.

'Rex?' the younger woman called out eventually. 'Oh, where art thou, Master Rex? 'Tis your sworn servant Juliet, here to perform any service at thy behest. And if thou couldst summon up a chicken nugget, verily I am starving.'

'Rex, Rex, it's time to vex, it's time to curse, it's time to hex!' the fairy thing chanted, making paper flower petals appear from his fingers. 'Let's make some sport, let's have some fun, let's poke your neighbours in the—'

'Puck!' the older woman chided, sending the fairy into a sulk.

'If Rex was here, he would have dug it,' he grumbled. 'And I too crave a chicken nugget.'

'I told you something terrible had happened,' moaned the skull, apparently also capable of speech. 'We're trapped! We're doomed! We're all going to die!'

'Peace, Yorick!' commanded the older woman, looking straight at Will, who was yet to regain the power of speech. 'My name is Lady Macbeth. Who art thou, craven youth? And wither is Rex? Is he murdered in cold blood? Have you done away with him in some foul plot? Are you, even now, tortured with guilt at your fiendish plot? Because this I can work with.'

Will stood, blinking his eyes, before remembering that his lips could still move.

'Er . . . hi,' he said eventually to the tiny people in the book. 'I'm Will. Who are you? What is going on? Why are you here? And do I need a doctor?'

It made sense to him to get all the most important questions out first.

'Will?' said Lady Macbeth with a raised eyebrow. Despite the fact that Will could have squashed her with the palm of his hand, something about this woman told him he should do what she said. She made him feel like his head teacher had just walked in the room. 'And what of your family name, young Will? What is your bloodline?'

'Er . . . well . . . you know Rex, right?' Will proffered, still utterly bewildered.

'Even him,' Lady Macbeth nodded, which Will figured meant yes.

'Well, I'm his grandson,' he replied. 'Will Davenant.

And I have absolutely no idea what is going on.'

The bizarre visitors looked amongst themselves with sad glances.

'Then it is as we feared,' Lady Macbeth said eventually. 'Rex has passed into the gloomy shade of death.'

'Verily, this is a dark day,' Juliet sobbed, picking up the skull – Yorick, was it? – and hugging it to her.

'Told you he was dead,' Yorick groaned. 'Everyone dies. We're all going to die.'

'Perhaps our Rex but slumbers here,' said Puck quietly. 'Sleep well, dear friend. We'll keep you near.'

Puck floated up from the book, although he could only go so far. As he floated up, Will could make out a string of golden words still tethering him to the page. The fairy hovered above the book, held a hand to his lips and gently blew a wisp of smoke. It danced and circled around the room, splitting into long silver strands that snaked through the air until they settled in the evening glow to form a picture of what was clearly Rex's face.

It hung in the middle of the room as the Shakespeareans bowed their heads in a moment's silent tribute. Will stared at the hazy image – it was the first picture of his adult grandfather he had seen. Even in the wisps of smoke, he could mark the resemblance that Olivia seemed so sure about. They had the same eyes, the same nose – although Will had a lot more hair. It was bizarre, seeing this shadow of the man before him. And as it faded away, the three figures who had a body either curtseyed or bowed. It was a touching tribute. If totally wasted on his loser grandfather. There was a respectful pause.

'See you, Rex,' Yorick said mournfully. 'And don't worry. The first four hundred years are the worst.'

A sad silence fell over the group. Will felt the urge to say something.

'Er . . . sorry for your loss?' he offered, as countless people had said to him. 'Now can someone please tell me what is happening here?'

The group looked amongst one another, confused.

'You know not, Master William?' Juliet enquired. 'Rex didn't tell you?'

'He didn't,' Will said stiffly. 'This is very much my "knowing not" face. What's going on – who are you?'

They all looked at a loss as to what to say. But Lady Macbeth took a step forward.

'It is not who we are that matters, child,' she offered. 'It is who *you* are.'

Will considered this for a moment.

'Nope, still not getting it,' he said after a brief silence.

'Sweet Will,' said Juliet softly. 'With your grandfather's passing, your family's great legacy passes on to you.'

Will felt a stir of excitement. Legacy? That meant money, right?

'You, like your grandfather before you, and all your male bloodline before him, now have the duty and care of this enchanted tome,' said Lady Macbeth, gesturing to the book surrounding her. 'You, young William Davenant, are now the Bard.'

She said it with such grandeur, Will took a second to consider her words. Something flashed in his mind. The Bard? Wasn't that what was written on the back of Rex's photograph? But even so . . .

'Nah. Still nothing,' he said.

Juliet walked to the edge of the book and sat down, dangling her legs over the edge of the pages. Her steps left a trail of word-prints across the page – like Puck, it appeared she too was joined to the book – any part of her touching it was connected to it by a thin string of words, which rose from the page like threads of honey with her every movement.

'Allow me to enlighten you, sweet William,' she said kindly. 'You, Rex, your whole family, you are all direct descendants of the greatest writer the world has ever known.'

Will considered this.

'I'm related to Stan Lee?' he said, excited at the connection to his comic-creating hero.

'No!' Yorick moaned. 'Until the day you die – and be warned, that'll probably be a lot sooner than you think – you're the great-great-great-great-keep-on-going-with-the-greats-great-great-grandson of William Shakespeare!'

The weight of this pronouncement sat heavily on Will's mind.

'Seriously?' Will spluttered disappointedly. 'The guy who wrote the weird fairy play?'

'The man who wrote of joy and tears, whose stories last four hundred years,' Puck chipped in, turning himself into an image that Will recognized from school – a balding guy with a moustache holding a quill. William Shakespeare. And he was Will's great-something grandfather.

As if he didn't have enough problematic relatives.

'OK, so, there's that,' Will said slowly. 'But . . . how does that make weird people – no offence – jump out of a book?'

'None taken,' Juliet said. 'Master Shakespeare had three children with his wife, Anne. But there was another child. And his name was William Davenant.'

Will couldn't help but startle at this. That was his name. Weird.

'Master Shakespeare could not acknowledge his child in his lifetime – but he gave him a gift,' said Lady Macbeth, gesturing to the book around her. 'The power to summon his characters from the pages of this particular book, the only one of its kind.'

'All the men in your family have had this gift handed down through the generations,' Juliet added enthusiastically. 'And now, Master William, as a man of the Davenant line – it is yours.'

Will considered this.

'But I don't understand,' he said, allowing some logic into the situation. 'My Uncle Claude is Rex's son – shouldn't he be . . . ?'

'Oh, come on, Will, it's not that hard – you've got the book, you're now the Bard,' Puck huffed.

Lady Macbeth slowly raised her hands and the pages of the book flicked over them, closing the page on the forest scene and creating a moving rainbow of paper over the characters' heads until the book rested on the title page. Lady M gestured to the inside of the leather cover, which was inscribed with long columns of Davenant names. There was an Alexander, several Georges, a whole host of Bills, Wills and Williams and even a Hubert. Rex was there. And under him, in what Will now knew to be his grandfather's handwriting, was Will.

'He chose you,' Juliet said softly. 'As every Bard has chosen his successor.'

That was even more weird. Why would Rex do that? They didn't even know each other. If he were honest,

Will had been secretly hoping that his grandfather might have left him and his mum some money so they could go on his dream holiday. But a magical book?

This wasn't going to get them to Universal Studios.

'Rex's whole life is within these pages,' said Lady Macbeth, signalling the documents stuffed inside.

'Rex's whole life is all over this flat,' Will corrected, thinking of the mountain of paperwork still waiting for him.

'But he saved the best stories for here,' Juliet pointed out, making the pages flick over them again until they opened at the page of *Romeo and Juliet.* A medieval Italian townscape sprung up around the small characters, a cobbled square surrounded by pastel buildings with colourful balconies, an ornate fountain flowing at its heart.

'Ah,' Juliet sighed, looking around the scene. 'You could live a long and happy life here.'

Puck picked up a photo that was tucked between the pages. It was an old picture of a bride and groom. Will pulled it out and turned it around. Like the picture of Rex as a boy, his grandfather had captioned it.

The Happiest Day
Me and Violet
Our wedding
Sept 1966

'Glad he was a fan of some couples,' Will snorted, stuffing the picture back into the book. 'So . . . where are all the others? I mean, Shakespeare wrote a bunch of plays, right? So there must be more of you?'

'There were,' Juliet sighed. 'But over the centuries, they have all been liberated.'

'Probably dead now,' Yorick muttered.

'They are not!' Juliet chided with a smile. 'Shylock runs an extensive chain of betting shops. Titus Andronicus just got his second Michelin star. Hamlet shares his musings most successfully on the Tik of the Tok. And I believe Troilus and Cressida were recently victorious on the *Island of Love* . . .'

'Hold on, liberated?' Will asked. 'Set free from the book, you mean? How?'

'By the Bard, of course,' Lady Macbeth pronounced. 'It is his duty. Successive generations have done theirs. And now, young William – it is your time.'

'Duty? My time? I don't understand,' Will said, because he really didn't.

Puck flew as far from the book as his word-leash would allow. The low sunbeams were creating shadows on Will's bedroom floor. Puck waved his arms, conducting this light and shade with his fingers. It danced around on the floor until moving images started to form like a movie on his bedroom carpet. A young man was scribbling away with a quill – Will figured it must be Shakespeare. As he wrote, golden swirls emanated from his page, just as they had done from the *Complete Works*, crafting people and places all around him.

'When Master Shakespeare created us,' Juliet narrated over the images, 'he never meant for us to stay bound within these pages. That's why he wrote. He wanted all his characters to come to life.'

'As he handed this book to his son, that was his dying wish,' Lady Macbeth continued. 'That his stories would live on, that they would take on a life of their own. And so that has been the Bard's responsibility. To release us from these pages. To keep his stories alive.'

The images dissolved back into the shadow.

'So, how does that . . . how do I do it?' Will asked, his brain still struggling to make sense of it all.

'Is it not obvious?' Juliet giggled.

'Not really,' Will admitted.

'Why, Master Will, it's time for glory,' said Puck, flying over and releasing a stream of golden words around his head. 'You, the Bard, must tell your story.'

Will stopped to think about this as the enchanted letters danced before his eyes.

'Nope,' he said. 'Still don't get it.'

'It's simple, child,' said Lady Macbeth impatiently. 'Since the dawn of time, stories have illuminated the human soul. They take us to different times and places. They tell of things we have not seen and reflect the things we have. They are as vital to being alive as breathing air.'

'No need to rub it in,' Yorick grumbled, to a disapproving glare from Lady M.

'They are also outstanding for getting people to do precisely what you want,' she continued. 'But that's a lesson for another day.'

'You see, young Will,' said Juliet, holding her tiny hands to her tiny heart. 'This is what Master Shakespeare always knew, what he realized when he created us all.'

'What was that?' asked Will, his brow furrowed with confusion.

The young woman gestured to the words that surrounded her and smiled.

'That stories set us free,' she whispered.

Will sat back and let her words sink in. He kinda got it. When he was reading his comics, or drawing his pictures, it was true – it felt like he was taken somewhere else, somewhere outside of his head, somewhere outside of his life. But it was one thing feeling like he was fighting with the Avengers. Quite another to be freeing magical characters from a magical book.

'So, what was Rex's story?' he asked. 'Who did he free?'

There was an awkward shuffle amongst the characters.

'His years were long and life was old,' Puck eventually spoke up. 'But Rex D left his tale untold . . .'

'We are the final three,' Lady Macbeth interrupted.

'Oi!' Yorick moaned. 'Check your head count!'

'We are the final four,' Lady M corrected. 'Master Rex never finished his story. So we are still here. And so now, child, it is down to you.'

'Hold on, wait a minute, Rex is dead,' Will said, regretting his candour a bit when he saw the Shakespeareans flinch. 'That seems like a pretty solid end to a story.'

'You're telling me,' Yorick huffed.

The other characters looked amongst each other, as though they didn't quite know what to say.

'A final breath is not the end,' Puck said gently. 'His story lives in you, my friend.'

'And so, young William, we need you,' Juliet implored. 'Help us, please. And we will do everything in our power to help you.'

'Help?' Will asked. 'What do you mean, help? Not to be rude or anything, but I've got socks bigger than you and you're tied to a book, so . . .'

'We are the Bard's sworn protectors and companions,' Lady Macbeth said. 'We are here to support you, to guide you, to come to your aid, to help you commit foul murders, whatever you require.'

'To bring some joy, some laughs, some art!' Puck cheered, taking flight around the book and showering it with butterflies. 'Let's start by having a giant—'

'Will?' came Mary's voice through the locked door, causing his heart to hammer in his damp chest. 'Who are you talking to?'

'Er . . . myself,' said Will in a panic. 'I'm, er, thinking of auditioning for the school play next term and I wanted to practise some voices.'

There was a silence. Surely his mum wouldn't buy this. She knew he hated his school and everyone in it.

'That's amazing,' she said softly. 'It's great to hear you want to get more involved. And you sound great – that bossy old woman voice is perfect.'

Will looked down at fuming Lady Macbeth and had to stifle a smile.

'But get yourself ready,' Mary continued. 'We need to get Angela's dinner down us before the election. Hurry up.'

'Don't eat that woman's food, refrain!' Puck warned in a whisper. 'Or you'll be bunged like a clogged-up drain.'

'Be right there!' Will called out, before turning again to the small cast of Shakespearean characters atop his book. 'OK, listen, I'm sorry for your troubles, truly. But

I've got kind of a lot going on here myself, so I'm going to have to pass.'

He started to close the book, much to the objection of the characters. Lady Macbeth, Juliet and Puck shot up and raised their palms against the closing cover, Yorick shuffling himself into the corner to wedge the pages open. Will felt them pushing back and it gave him a slightly sicky feeling in his gut.

'Tarry, Master Will!' Lady Macbeth commanded. 'Think on it. We only live while these pages are open! To keep a book closed is to deny its characters life!'

'I'm sorry,' Will apologized, and he meant it. 'Truly. But I've got enough problems of my own.'

And with a guilty slam, he closed the *Complete Works.*

The moment the covers made contact, the light from the pages immediately extinguished. As it dimmed, that same picture dropped out of it, of Rex holding the book as a younger man. So perhaps that's what the smile was about? Had his grandfather just discovered that he was the Bard too?

Wow.

So he and Rex had one whole thing in common.

A ferocious knock on the door pulled him out of his stupor.

'William Davenant!' came Mary's strident voice. 'If you're not out here in two minutes, so help me, I am eating this whole lasagne myself!'

'Coming!' Will cried, stuffing the book under his wardrobe. 'I was just, er, reading.'

'You? Reading a book?' Mary scoffed outside the door. 'Now I know you're lying. Get your butt out here, kiddo. We've got an election to get to.'

CHAPTER V

Uneasy Lies the Head . . .

It being another warm evening, the election was to take place outside in the gardens. By the time Will and Mary had eaten Angela's lasagne – which, if Will were entirely honest, wasn't nearly as nice as it first appeared – a large number of people were already assembled on two sides of the lawn. They were sitting on garden chairs, deckchairs, dining chairs; a patchwork of furniture and families.

Even from his limited understanding of Arden Heights, Will could already see the division. The two sides of the lawn were entirely distinct, each talking happily within its own group, but no one venturing across the grass to join the other. The only things that travelled across the void were dirty looks and muttered insults. The Heights was two islands separated by a river of anger. Will wished he'd brought his sketch pad down. It would have made a good, if sad, picture. He didn't know which was Team For and Team Against. But he understood that this was a community in pieces.

Mary unfolded the picnic blanket she'd found in the linen cupboard, poured herself a glass of wine and handed Will a bottle of coke and a packet of crisps. They were just about to tuck into their snacks, when a small whirlwind cannoned across the lawn towards them.

'You can't sit there!' hissed Hurricane Ani. 'This is Team For territory! Come on, come over here, quick!'

She started to gather up the blanket, seemingly untroubled that Mary and Will were still sitting on it.

'Er, hi?!' said Mary, a smile playing on her lips. Will thought how often his mum used to smile. It was good to see it again.

'Hi!' said Ani brightly, not pausing from picking up their things. 'Let's go. I saved you some seats next to us.'

Ani grabbed everything around them and made to head for the other side of the lawn, before colliding with a ferocious woman with a cane who was striding in the opposite direction.

'Watch where you're going, girl!' the woman barked at her.

'Sorry, Ms Minola,' said Ani, trying a charming smile on the woman. It didn't work.

'Stay out of my way,' Ms Minola muttered as she marched towards the few chairs near the front that neither side seemed to have claimed.

'Oops! Anyhoo,' said Ani with a shrug, 'here's our spot.'

She gestured to where Ben was sitting next to three empty chairs. He glanced their way, but made no further acknowledgement of their existence.

'That's very kind,' Mary said hesitantly. 'Erm . . .'

'Ani,' Ani added with a grin, thrusting out her hand. 'My mum named me after her favourite singer. She used to sing me this song by her, "There Must Be an Angel"? She said it was about me. You'd probably know it. It's really old.'

Will groaned at Ani's lack of tact – his mum turning forty soon had made her super touchy about her age. But Mary just laughed.

'It's a lovely song,' she said. 'I remember when Elizabeth I and I used to listen to it back in the day.'

'Oh, that sounds fun,' said Ani cheerfully.

'But we'll sit here, thanks,' Mary said, shooting a look at Ben and repositioning the blanket. 'I'm sure your mum will want a seat anyway.'

'Nah, she's not here,' said Ani distractedly, looking around the gathering. 'She's a singer. She's doing a big concert in London.'

'I thought she was on tour?' Will asked.

'She is, duh!' Ani said witheringly. 'The London concert is on the tour, she'll probably sing that song.'

'And I thought your name was Anishka?'

'Can I borrow Will for a minute?' Ani asked Mary. 'I'd like to show him around.'

'Sure,' said Mary, raising her glass and settling on to her blanket. 'I've got everything I need right here.'

Will was about to ask if his mum was sure when he was unceremoniously dragged away by Ani.

'OK,' she gabbled. 'Pretty much everyone is here tonight, so here's the lowdown on Arden Heights.'

She took a breath. Will sensed it could be the last one for a while.

'So,' she began, 'this evil developer, Egeus, wants to buy all thirty-eight flats and turn the building into a posh hotel.'

'And?' shrugged Will. 'What's the big deal?'

Ani's face turned the colour of the setting sun.

'The big deal?!' she cried. 'The big deal?! The big deal is that this is a community!'

Will looked between the two enemy camps.

'Doesn't look like much of a community,' he said, gesturing to the gaping divide.

'Well, it was before Egeus ruined everything!' Ani raged. 'Some people have lived here all their lives – and intended to see out the rest of their days here! Most of the residents are elderly – to move now would be super traumatic for them. If the Egeus sale goes ahead, all the flats will be sold, so even those who want to stay will have to move!'

There was so much passion in Ani's voice.

And yet still Will didn't get it.

'So it *is* a big deal?' he confirmed.

'Look,' said Ani firmly. 'The bottom line is this. Ben found this old clause in the contracts all the flat owners have to sign – he's a fancy lawyer so he's good with this stuff. Arden Heights can't be sold if twenty or more flat owners object to the sale.'

'So . . . more than half?' said Will, doing the maths.

'Exactly,' Ani confirmed. 'On Friday, there's going to be a vote – those who want the development are Team For. Team Against are trying to stop it. To do that, we need to get twenty of thirty-seven flat owners to vote against. And right now, it's too close to call.'

'Hold on,' said Will, doing some more maths. 'You said there were thirty-eight flats?'

'There are only thirty-seven votes,' Ani explained. 'Caleb, the caretaker, doesn't get one as he gets to live in his flat for free. And because he's pond slime.'

'Yeah, I've had the pleasure,' Will replied. 'What's his deal?'

'Oh, he's been in a bad mood for, like, fifty years or something,' Ani said dismissively. 'I heard his younger brother stole their family business from him. The brother made a ton of money, Caleb mops floors, he's annoyed, yada, yada, get over it.'

Will looked over to the caretaker, whose face was etched into a miserable scowl. A wave of pity surged inside him. Someone taking more than their fair share? This he understood.

'If he was cheated, no wonder he's angry,' said Will. 'It's no fun living without money. Especially if it's rightfully yours.'

'All right, all right,' Ani said, and Will realized how fiercely he had spoken. 'Calm down. Anyway, we need twenty against votes to win. We know all the Kings are on our side . . .'

'The Kings?' Will asked.

'Oh, massive family, owns ten of the flats here,' Ani explained. 'They're always fighting about something, but they're all right. Look, that's them over there.'

Will looked over to a patch of lawn that had generations of the family across about twenty picnic blankets. Even from across the lawn he could hear them – there was bickering over food, children arguing over toys, a lot about politics . . .

'They're all fathers and sons and cousins,' said Ani, as

two little Kings raced passed them dressed up as animals. 'That's Henry, Henry, Richard, Henry, Henry, Henry, Richard, Henry, Henry and—'

'Let me guess,' grinned Will. 'Henry? Or Richard?'

Ani looked at him blankly.

'No. John,' she said. 'Duh.'

'My bad,' muttered Will, as a toy horse flew past his head.

'Anyway, they're all Team Against – their family has lived here for generations, so that's ten votes straight away,' said Ani as they moved around the garden. 'We're obviously against, as Angela and Julian must be – why stand for a residents' committee if the residents are about to be thrown out? – as well as that couple in 25 who are only ever here for less than a fortnight, so that's fourteen. However. We also know that those cousins in flat 38, the Nobles, are for, as is Coral in 32 – she's weird, follows Angela around like a lapdog, the wives who live at 22 – shame, they're great fun, but want to move to Windsor, the moody guy from 21, the divorcing couple in 31, the angry Greek guy in 28, and the twins – can't tell them apart – in flat 8.'

'Well, that's only . . . seven,' said Will. 'So you should be fine.'

'Eight,' said Ani darkly. 'There's another vote we're pretty sure about.'

'Who?' said Will.

'Flat 29,' Ani sighed. 'Yours.'

Will put the pieces together. Of course. Uncle Claude had sent them down to clear the flat up to sell it. To the developers. To make a quick buck. That made perfect sense. That was peak Claude.

'Listen, that's nothing to do with me and Mum, that's—'

'I know, chill,' Ani sighed. 'Ben told me your uncle owns the flat now? I knew Rex would never do that. He was awesome.'

'You . . . you knew him?' Will asked.

'Sure,' Ani shrugged. 'We all knew Rex. The Duke was such a dude. Everyone loved him.'

'Not everyone,' muttered Will.

'Anyway,' Ani continued, as another small King ran past in a tiger costume, 'everyone else is playing their cards close to their chest, so we don't know how they are voting. We just need to persuade six more flats on to Team Against, then we're set no matter what. I've identified our best bets: the gardening committee in flats 10, 14, 19 and 24 – if they don't kill each other first.'

'Oh, yeah, I got that,' Will smiled, thinking of the scene he'd witnessed on his way to the beach.

'Always the drama with that lot,' Ani sighed, rather dramatically. 'So the latest is that Rosie wants to go to this tea dance with Patrick on Thursday, but Hemie already asked him. Rosie is crazy into Patrick – she's been baking him her special Victoria sponge for months, thought it was a done deal, so she's mad with Hemie for . . . cutting her grass.'

'Er . . . OK,' Will answered, trying to make sense of the love quadrangle. 'So what do Patrick and Antoine want?'

Ani shrugged.

'I think they just like planting stuff,' she said. 'But I reckon if we can sort them all out, they'll all want to stay. There's also Monty in flat 11.'

Will followed Ani's pointing finger to a man staring sadly across the garden at a woman chatting with Angela.

'That's Sylvie from flat 34,' Ani explained. 'Used to be a jeweller, makes lovely jam. Monty's nuts about her and I think she likes him, but they're still not together. I can't get to the bottom of it. But I will.'

'Of course you will,' said Will, already getting a sense of Ani's boundless determination. 'So that's five. Who's the last one?'

Ani pointed to a woman sitting stiffly on a chair, giving disapproving looks to all her neighbours. This woman he'd already met.

'Ms Minola?' he questioned. 'Why her? She doesn't exactly look very happy to be here. None of them do.'

'Well, that's just it, genius,' Ani said, like it was the most obvious thing in the world. 'We make them all happy, they'll want to stay.'

'Sorry, we?' said Will, just as Caleb trudged to the front of the gathering and banged on the microphone, making it squeak horribly.

'All right, you lot, simmer down,' the caretaker barked at the Arden Heights residents, who slowly obeyed. 'Right, as the only non-voting resident – and why the one who cleans up after you sloppy so-and-sos shouldn't get a say, I dunno, but no one cares what I think – I'm in charge here. Two candidates have put themselves forward to head the residents' committee – Julian Gaius from flat 20 and Angela Dominante from flat 30.'

Angela and Julian stood up, waved amiably at everyone before shaking hands with a friendly laugh.

'As per the rules here at Arden Heights, each candidate will make a speech before everyone casts their vote on the papers provided,' Caleb growled. 'And I WILL be checking I get all me pencils back at the end. Angela, let's be having you.'

There was a smattering of applause from the residents as Angela walked confidently to the front with her notes.

'Hello, dears,' she said sweetly, as Will and Ani made their separate ways back to their parents. 'What an honour it is to stand before you. I know I won't be alone in missing our dear Rex tonight – but I'm delighted that his daughter Mary and grandson Phil are currently staying with us at the Heights.'

She gestured towards Mary, who gave an embarrassed wave of acknowledgement.

'This is awkward,' Mary said through gritted teeth, trying to discreetly put her wine down. 'Smile . . . Phil.'

Will quickly lifted his hand, before burying it in a bag of crisps. He didn't like people looking at him. He didn't want to be seen.

'I'm sure you'll all make them feel very welcome,' Angela said. 'And be tolerant as they learn the rules of our community. It's not their fault they don't know the bins should have gone out tonight. Although they do now.'

Angela nodded at them. Again, Will felt like he did around Lady Macbeth, like he was in trouble with a teacher.

'Anyhoo,' said Angela brightly, 'back to business. As you know, I am putting myself forward for head of our residents' committee. I have a deep and enduring love for Arden Heights and it would be my honour to serve.'

There was enthusiastic applause from a single member of the audience. Will figured that was Coral.

'Rex was a kind and understanding man,' Angela

began. 'His . . . latitude with our rules was admirable, but maybe not practical.'

'Hear, hear,' Coral shouted out.

'But I believe that rules are to be obeyed,' Angela said firmly. 'They may have been dead to Rex, but for me, they were merely asleep. Our community needs order, discipline and accountability. Without them, we face anarchy, chaos and disharmony.'

A tentative hand went up.

'Is this about the confusion with the rec room?' the man asked. 'Because I honestly thought skittles was on a Tuesday. I didn't realize that art club were drying their sculptures there. Or I wouldn't have thrown me ball at them.'

'No, no, no, Leon,' Angela chortled, her laugh sounding like an out-of-tune violin. 'Not at all. Although thank goodness you're such a poor shot, or Peri from flat 33 would have lost that delightful sculpture of himself. Naked.'

'It's art,' Peri insisted as Will heard his mother snort into her glass of wine.

'No, what I'm talking about is, while it is tempting to break the rules, it serves none of us any good to live in a lawless society. If elected your chair, I will bring discipline, order and consequence back to Arden Heights. There will be no guests without written permission.

There will be no ball games in the swimming pool. There will be no music after eight p.m. And there will be no towels on balconies. This is a residential dwelling. Not a party resort in . . . Ibiza!'

Coral gasped in horror at the very suggestion.

'And so,' Angela said, resuming the smile. 'A vote for me is a vote for Arden Heights becoming a place of order. A place of safety. And above all, a place of justice. I'm Angela Dominante. And this is my pledge to you.'

Angela finished her speech with a triumphant flourish, in anticipation of rapturous applause. And she got it.

From Coral.

'Brava!' her mate cheered across the polite smattering of clapping. 'Angela for chair! Angela for chair! Angela for chair!'

She tried to encourage the other residents into a chant. It didn't work.

'Wow,' Will whispered to his mum as Coral sat down sheepishly. 'That was . . . intense.'

'Certainly was,' Mary said hesitantly. 'And, honestly, her lasagne wasn't even that good.'

Will smiled. His mum could be so awesome. When she wasn't being . . . a mum.

'All right, settle down,' Caleb called over the slightly scandalized chatter coming from the residents. 'Julian, go.'

Julian – a man who looked straight out of a catalogue

for over-seventies clothing – walked to the front and smiled brightly at everyone. Unlike Angela, he was not holding notes, but he did look incredibly nervous as he faced his fellow residents.

'Friends! Residents! Countrymen! Lend me your ears!' he began with a big smile. This made all the adults laugh. Will wasn't really sure why.

'Gosh, tough act to follow there, Angela,' he said amiably. 'And we'd be lucky to have you.'

He looked for agreement amongst the crowd. He didn't get much.

'Well, not sure I've got quite such a . . . powerful message,' Julian bumbled. 'But I was a great admirer – and I hope I can say, friend – of the Duke.'

Julian looked kindly over towards Mary. Will heard his mother's breath catch.

'And I know that the quality he valued over all else was kindness,' Julian continued. Will tried, unsuccessfully, to stifle a huff, earning him a poke in the ribs from Mary. All these people telling him how a man that had frozen out his own daughter was such a great guy. It wasn't right.

'And so, I suppose, if I have a pitch, it is that,' Julian continued, 'I want ours to be a kind and inclusive place, just as Rex ensured it was. After all, it was him who fought to make sure everyone was welcome here. The covenants of Arden Heights didn't always allow for anyone to live here – the Duke made sure that no matter how you looked, who you loved or what you believed, you were welcome at the Heights. He wanted anyone and everyone to find their home here. And that's what I want too. I'm aware that there are issues that divide us. But there are so many more that unite us. If, as I hope, Arden Heights is still ours a few days hence, I would like us to listen more than we shout. To consider more than we condemn. And to understand, even where we don't agree. Because Arden Heights is our home. And we are a family. And while families don't always see eye to eye—'

'You got that right!' shouted one of the Kings, probably a Henry. There was a ripple of laughter around the gardens.

'—we can still all muddle along together,' said Julian. 'So there you have it. I love being part of this family – and I want you all to love it too. I'm Julian Gaius. And I need a drink.'

No sooner had Julian finished than the crowd erupted with applause, some residents even taking to their feet to express their admiration. Will found himself joining in – as speeches go, it wasn't as boring as they usually were. He didn't generally take any interest in votes, that was something that adults did, like laundry and shopping and earning money. But if he had to call this election – Julian had already won. Will glanced over at Angela. She was still smiling. There was no warmth in it, though. He figured that Angela knew she'd been beaten too.

'All right, enough chatter,' said Caleb gruffly as a herd of small Kings nearly knocked him flying. 'You all had a ballot paper put through your doors this morning. Cast your vote, stick it in the box, I'll count them and then we can all get on with our lives. Also, subscriptions are due today – there's a bowl by the ballot box. And remember: PENCILS!'

The residents all delved into pockets, handbags and backpacks to pull out their forms and their money. Mary had brought their paper down in her bag and held it out for Will to see.

'Who do you think Uncle Claude would vote for?' she whispered to Will. 'It's his flat – it should be his vote.'

'Oh, Angela, for sure,' Will said convincingly. 'They speak the same language. I think it's called—'

'Thank you!' his mother interrupted before the rudeness could fall out of his mouth. 'I agree. Uncle Claude would definitely vote for Angela. So let's do the right thing.'

She looked at her son and winked mischievously, before putting a massive tick next to Julian's name.

'Take it over to the box for me, kiddo,' she said, handing the paper over and leaning back on the blanket, tilting her face to the evening sun. 'You don't have a dog and bark yourself.'

Will took the paper with a scowl. He'd never entirely understood what that phrase meant. But the upshot was always the same: he had to do something his mum didn't want to do.

By the time he reached the table, there was already a small queue of residents waiting to post their votes in the makeshift ballot box. He joined it, just as Ani cannoned up to him, apparently oblivious to the huffs and tuts of the residents behind him.

'So, who did you vote for?' she said at a volume that could wake the dead.

Will looked uncomfortably around him.

'It's a secret,' he whispered back.

Ani laughed out loud.

'No, it's not!' she scoffed. 'Anyone in their right mind is going to vote for Julian. Did you hear Angela's speech?'

Will flinched at her indiscretion. As did Angela, who was walking straight towards them.

'Hello, children,' she beamed. 'Are you having fun? Did you enjoy my choccie cake?'

Will was wondering how best to respond, when Ani saved him the trouble.

'The chocolate cake was all right, thanks, Angela – although my guts have been bunged up like the recycling skip on bin day,' she declared. 'But it's not going to buy our vote. That's not how democracy works. We've voted for Julian, because we think that's what's best for Arden Heights.'

Will withered internally. On the one hand, he admired Ani. There was a lot to be said for saying exactly what you meant. But on the other . . . it was really, incredibly awkward.

'Well, dearie,' said Angela with that cold smile again. 'Thank you for your candour. How . . . refreshing. And how are you, young Philip? Enjoying the evening?'

Will could feel Ani's eyes boring into him. But he couldn't meet Angela's.

'Lovely lasagne,' he muttered. 'Thanks a lot.'

He went to wipe off the slight sweat that had blossomed on his brow. But in his nervousness, he accidentally dropped his voting paper. Which, of course, landed face up on the grass. Angela glanced at the clear vote for her competition.

'Well, I hope it helped,' she said coldly. 'It's so important to be a good neighbour. Watch where you're going, children!'

Two Kings, one dressed like an elephant, the other a lion, simply laughed as they rampaged past. Angela narrowed her eyes and moved towards another resident in the queue.

'Brrrrr,' said Ani, visibly shuddering. 'She's got such a weird energy. And why didn't you correct her about your name?'

Will watched Angela work her way up the line. Ani was right. There was something . . . off about her.

'Niceness and goodness don't always go hand in hand,' his dad used to say.

'Doesn't matter,' he mumbled.

'Yes, it does,' Ani insisted. 'You have a right to be called by your actual name. Speak up.'

Will was about to say something.

But he didn't.

The line shuffled forward and Will and Ani put their papers in the box.

'PENCILS!' Caleb growled at them, making them both jump. 'Then clear off!'

Will handed his pencil over and was about to return to his mum when Ani stopped him.

'Where's your dad?' Ani asked, even more bluntly than she usually did.

Will took a small breath. This sentence never got any easier.

'He died,' he said quietly. 'Just over two years ago.'

He waited for the awkward silence, the muttered 'I'm sorry', the head tilt, the hand on his shoulder – any of the standard responses that tended to follow this reveal.

‘Oh,’ Ani simply replied. ‘So Mary’s single, then?’

Will couldn’t help laughing.

‘Er . . . yeah,’ he said. ‘That’s kinda how it works.’

‘Interesting,’ said Ani, looking over to where Mary was chatting on the blanket with Sylvie. ‘She’d be good for Ben.’

Will tried not to choke on the swig of drink he’d just taken.

‘WHAT?!’ he spat. ‘You’re joking! I had a ringside seat this morning when they met. It didn’t exactly feel like a love story.’

‘All the more reason,’ said Ani thoughtfully.

Will was trying to formulate a response when Caleb’s aggressive clap interrupted the chatter.

‘Oi!’ he shouted. ‘So I’ve counted the votes – we have a result.’

The cloud of bodies in the gardens returned to their seats. Julian and Angela moved to the front, once again exchanging a friendly handshake and some smiled words.

‘Well, this won’t take long,’ Caleb announced. ‘I’ve counted ’em twice, but it don’t make no difference. We had thirty-four votes, two abstentions, one vote for the Monster Raving Loony Party and another paper with some chewing gum inside. But the result is as plain as the spots on me bum. With thirty votes, the winner . . .

is Julian Gaius.'

Will watched the two candidates. Julian looked genuinely delighted and surprised. Angela tried to look genuinely anything. But her eyes were cold. So, so cold . . .

'Thank you, my friends,' said Julian, coming to the front and dulling down the rapturous applause. 'This is an incredible honour, and one I shall cherish. There is much to do here – but the first order of business is clear. The vote as to whether Egeus can purchase our block is in two short days. Nothing is set in stone and everyone must of course do what is right for them. But let me state my case clearly here and now. As far as I'm concerned, this is our home. This is our community. And I will work tirelessly to ensure it stays that way. I am AGAINST the Egeus development.'

There were cheers from some and stony silences from others. There it was again, Will observed. A chasm of division.

'And may I please also take this opportunity to thank Angela for her dignified campaign and personal friendship?' Julian continued. 'For my first act as chair, I would like to propose her to be my deputy. I know she will be a great support to me in the coming months.'

This was met with a less enthusiastic round of applause. But if Angela noticed, she didn't respond. She came straight to the front, practically pushing Julian out of the way and snatching the microphone from his hand.

'Well, thank you, Julian – and I would like to officially accept the role,' she said, although Will was sure it hadn't actually been decided. 'The Egeus development is an emotive and contentious issue. I look forward to all sides being represented.'

'Hmmm,' Ani muttered next to Will. 'Don't let that fence post chafe your bum, Angela.'

Will wasn't entirely sure what Ani meant. But her face told a story of its own.

'All right, you lot,' Caleb barked over the microphone. 'Make sure you tidy up after yourselves! I don't wanna repeat of the Bonfire Night BBQ. I was picking up burnt bangers for days! And when you've packed yourselves up, you can all just clear—'

'AAAAAARRRRGGGGHHHHHH!' screamed another of the King children, this one dressed like a bear.

'AAAAAARRRRGGGHHHHHHHHH!' Caleb screamed back, as the bear chased him off the lawn, accompanied by its many animal-clad cousins.

'Right,' Ani declared. 'We need to step up our campaign. We need twenty against votes to save Arden Heights. Tomorrow we target Ms Minola, Monty and the gardening committee.'

'Again with the "we",' Will objected. 'This is nothing

to do with me. I'm not getting involved.'

Ani fixed her piercing blue stare at Will.

'Oh, aren't you?' she said. 'Your grandfather fought hard to save this place. Don't you want to carry on his work?'

Will paused and looked at his feet.

'I didn't know Rex,' he said. 'I don't know anything about him.'

Ani scrumpled up her face.

'Why not?' she asked. Will sighed. She actually had no boundaries.

'There was a fight . . . I dunno,' Will shrugged. 'But my mum and him haven't spoken since before I was born.'

'OK,' said Ani, her bright eyes calculating a new angle. 'But this uncle of yours, Clive?'

'Claude,' Will corrected.

'Well, he sounds like a massive poo,' she announced.

Will couldn't help but laugh again. He'd never met anyone who said exactly what they thought all the time. It was growing on him.

'Yeah,' he said. 'He really is.'

'Well, then,' she whispered, leaning in, her eyes dancing like a pixie. 'The sale of the flats stands to make each resident a bunch of money.'

'Great,' groaned Will. 'Because Claude deserves some more.'

'Unless,' Ani twinkled, 'the development is voted down. Then he'd get nothing. Imagine that? And imagine if you were part of the reason it happened?'

Will did. He imagined how outraged his uncle would be about losing yet more easy money that he hadn't worked for. He'd be furious. He'd be frustrated. He'd be miserable.

He looked into Ani's sparkling blue eyes.

'Count me in,' he smiled.

CHAPTER VI

Though She Be but Little . . .

An eventful day led to a deep night's sleep for Will – so much so that his brain had to climb over several thoughts before fully waking up. How were he and Ani going to persuade the floating voters to save Arden Heights? And why was she asking about his mum and dad? Would he and Mum ever sort through Rex's papers? How would Uncle Claude punish him if Will lost him the money from the sale of the flat?

And then, finally . . .

Was it really OK that he had imprisoned some tiny people in the *Complete Works of William Shakespeare*?

Will looked guiltily at the book he had shoved under the wardrobe the previous day. In his haste, he hadn't noticed that a folded piece of paper had fallen out from the pages. Will reached out from his bed to pick it up and was about to tuck it back in, when a photograph fell out of it. The faces made the breath stick in his chest.

It was his dad. And his mum. And, technically, given the size of his mum's belly – him.

They looked so happy. So young. So . . . incredibly badly dressed, millennials had some weird fashion sense. Will had seen the picture before. It had been in a frame in their old house before they'd had to move to Claude's. His uncle had made them put all their things in the loft. There was no space for their memories at Uncle Claude's. There was barely space for them. As he looked at his parents' joyful faces, Will struggled as he always did with memories of his father. They were happy and sad all at once, each cancelling the other out until he felt nothing but numb.

Will opened the piece of paper. It was a letter. And he recognized the handwriting. It was his mum's.

'Morning, kiddo!' Mary yelled, knocking loudly on his door. 'You awake?'

Will's groggy head startled.

'I am now,' he groaned.

'Excellent!' said Mary breezily. 'Ani's here. Are you decent?'

'No!' Will cried, clutching the blanket around his body in a panic. It had been another hot night and he'd slept only in his underwear – no one could see him like this.

'Give me a minute.'

'OK,' Mary replied and he could hear the smile in her voice. 'Get your trousers on. And hurry up!'

'Sure,' said Will, holding the note in his hand. Despite the fact that Ani was waiting, he couldn't quite resist reading it anyway:

Papa,

I know you're still angry with me for the way I left. But new life is on the way and I hope with it, a new start for us all.

I'm having a baby, Papa! A boy! We're going to call him William. William Davenant. Your grandson.

We're at the address above. And we'd love to hear from you.

All our love,
Mary, Leo (& William)
xxx

Will didn't understand. Rex had completely disapproved of his parents' relationship. So why had he kept this? He felt the rage ignite inside him again. His mum had tried to – how did she put it? – extend an olive branch. And his stupid grandfather hadn't even bothered taking it. He was such a—

'Oi, Davenant, get a shift on!' Ani shouted, hammering at his door.

Will took a breath, tossed his blanket off and yanked on some trousers. The summer wasn't showing any signs of letting up and he looked longingly at the T-shirts his mum had packed for him.

But then he caught a glimpse of himself in the mirror. And reached for the jumper he had worn for the previous two days.

By the time he opened his door, Ani and his mum were deep in chat in the front room.

'Could you believe Angela's speech?' Ani said scandalously. 'What was that about?'

'I know, right?' said Mary enthusiastically. 'That was next-level weird—'

'And don't be taken in by her lasagne,' Ani said with a frown. 'I don't want to be rude, but you'll need dynamite to shift it from your—'

'I KNOW, RIGHT?' Mary repeated, reaching in for a high five, which was enthusiastically returned by her new young friend. 'Oh, hey, Will – nice of you to join us.'

She and Ani exchanged a smirking look that Will didn't entirely understand and certainly didn't like. Ani pulled Mary in for a selfie and posted it on her phone.

'For my mum,' Ani explained. 'She loves to know what I'm doing.'

'She must be missing you terribly,' Mary said sympathetically.

'Oh, she really is,' Ani said brightly. 'She called me from Paris this morning and–'

'I thought she was in London?' Will asked, his tired brain still waking up.

'The tour moves around a lot!' Ani said like he was an idiot. 'Geez, Mary – is he always this slow or did he leave his brain in his other jeans?'

'Nah,' said Will's mum. 'He'd have to change his trousers for that.'

'OK, then,' he interrupted, very keen to split this unholy alliance up. 'Come on, Ani – we've got stuff to do.'

'Oh, good!' said Mary happily. 'You two have plans? Another trip to the beach?'

It was on the edge of Will's lips to agree and say that, yes, they were just heading to the beach. It was so much easier than explaining the truth, which his mother would certainly have opinions about . . .

'No,' Ani said plainly. 'We're going to visit some of the residents and try to persuade them to vote against the Egeus development.'

Will winced. Why did Ani have to say everything so entirely–

'What a great idea,' his mum gasped admiringly. 'It would be so sad to see this place turn into another faceless development. It's . . . it means a lot. To a lot of people.'

Will watched a strange look pass over Mary's face. It really hadn't occurred to him that, whilst this was certainly a complicated place for her, it might have once been a happy one. He wondered how she was feeling about Arden Heights being erased entirely from her life. Just because she hadn't been to it for a while, at least it had always been there. Mary must have stories. And he wanted to hear them.

'Well, we need to get on with it. Thanks for the drink,' said Ani, putting her glass of water down and giving Mary a hug that caught her off guard.

'Oh, well . . . you're welcome,' laughed Will's mum, taking Ani into her arms and returning the cuddle. 'Any time.'

'Right,' said Ani, pulling away and yanking a clipboard and a pencil out of the backpack slung over her shoulder. 'I have an itinerary for today. Mary, is it OK if we have a meeting in Will's room? I don't want to disturb your work.'

'Go for it,' sighed Will's mum, looking hopelessly at the mountain of boxes as Ani barged past Will. 'I'm not going anywhere.'

Will sighed. Was all this really such a good idea? Crossing Uncle Claude? And there was so much to do here. He didn't want Ani to know what he was thinking, so he—

'Stop pulling that face,' she said, marching past him into his bedroom. 'If the wind changes, you'll stay like that.'

Will looked helplessly towards his mum, who simply shrugged her shoulders with an impish grin and went back to her boxes.

'Ha!' said Ani as she shut the door to Will's bedroom behind her. 'We've got the same room. Except mine has a lot fewer cardigans . . .'

'I'm just happy to have a bed I don't have to fold up,' Will muttered, before realizing that wouldn't make sense to Ani. 'At my Uncle Claude's, I sleep on a sofa bed. Next to the washing machine.'

'What?' Ani exclaimed. 'Rex said your uncle was loaded and has a massive house. Why don't you get your own room?'

'You'd have to ask him,' Will said, trying to clear some space on the bed for her to sit down. He picked up the small pile of clothes his mum had left and moved over to the chest of drawers to see if there was anywhere to put them.

'So we've got a lot to do today,' Ani began officiously. 'If we're going to persuade Ms Minola, Monty and the gardening committee to stay at Arden Heights, we're going to have to find out more about them. Oh, this is cool! I love these.'

'What?' asked Will absently, moving yet more cardigans to make room for his clothes.

'Shakespeare's plays,' he heard Ani reply before feeling his heart fall into his stomach. 'I think *Much Ado About Nothing* is my favourite. Wow, this book must be centuries old – what's all this stuff inside it?'

Will spun around in terror to see Ani holding the *Complete Works* on her lap. Her fingers were curled around the cover—

'NO!' he shouted, dropping the clothes and diving across the room to shut the book.

Had Will thought about it a second longer, he would have realized he didn't need to. He alone was the Bard. The book only responded to him. He could have let Ani happily flick through it, no harm done.

But he didn't.

Instead, he hurled himself headlong at Ani and the book, grabbing it just as she opened the front cover. And no sooner had his fingers made contact with the paper, the gold letters started wisping out of the pages.

'What . . .what's happening?!' Ani cried, dropping the open book on the floor as the room filled with swirling text.

Will tried to find some of his own words. But how could he explain something he didn't really understand himself?

The glistening letters floated around the room, dancing and whispering as they became words, then sentences, then characters. Ani's face froze in bewilderment as she watched them settle into their tiny Shakespearean forms. Lady M, Juliet, Puck and Yorick gradually took centre stage on the page, this time in Ancient Egypt, judging by the sand and pyramids.

'Master William!' Juliet exclaimed in delight, dancing around the page. 'You came back! I knew you would!'

'I didn't,' Yorick sighed. 'I thought you'd just leave us here until we wasted away.'

'Hmmm,' said Lady Macbeth grimly. 'I've spent all night devising foul murders for you. Such a waste.'

'To see you back is such a joy!' cheered Puck, whizzing up into the air to shower both Will and Ani with paper petals. 'And who's your friend, dressed like a boy?'

'Ah, you must be Will's wife!' Juliet exclaimed, clapping her hands gleefully. 'It's a pleasure to meet you!'

'My wife?' Will spat. 'We're thirteen years old!'

'Um . . . sorry to interrupt the wedding plans,' stammered Ani, her eyes flitting between the animated characters on the book. 'But would someone mind explaining to me what the very . . . heck . . . is going on here? And explaining to feather-face over there that girls can wear short hair and trousers, thanks.'

Everyone looked expectantly at Will. All except

Yorick, who was facing the wrong way.

'Don't mind me,' the skull moped, shuffling himself around. 'I may as well not be here.'

'Keep an eye on her,' Lady Macbeth whispered to Yorick. 'I don't trust her.'

'Er, hi?' said Ani with a sarcastic wave. 'I'm right here.'

'Look, I don't really get it,' said Will running a hand through his hair. 'But somehow . . . I'm related to Shakespeare, so I've got this magic book.'

'O . . . K . . .' Ani said, poking Yorick's skull and receiving a teeth gnash for her trouble. 'And what does that mean?'

'It means we can finally be free!' Juliet sang, raising her hands to the heavens. 'Master Will is going to liberate us!'

'Er, hold on, I thought we'd discussed this,' Will interrupted.

'Liberate you?' Ani probed. 'Liberate you from what?'

'This, wench,' Lady Macbeth said impatiently, gesturing to the book around her. 'These pages. We are trapped here until the Bard frees us with his—'

'His?' Ani interrupted. 'What if the Bard is a woman?'

'That's your top line here?' Will whispered. 'With the, y'know, magical book and everything?'

'It will never be,' said Juliet, shaking her head. 'Only a man can inherit the gift.'

'Master Shakespeare was a peerless observer of the human condition,' Lady M sighed. 'But even he had his blind spots.'

'This is . . . This is . . . This is . . . huge!' Ani blustered.

'I know, right?' Will said quietly, trying to shush her. 'And so you can see why I've told them that I can't help – I've already got a load of stuff to do.'

'You cannot leave us here to rot!' Puck implored. 'Fair maid! Please kick him up the—'

'What?!' Ani cried. 'You're . . . you're going to leave them here? Stuck in this book? Trapped? Imprisoned forever?'

'OK, when you put it like that, it doesn't sound great,' Will acknowledged. 'But—'

'But nothing!' said Ani ferociously. 'You can't do this to them!'

'I kinda can,' Will said from the corner of his mouth.

'No, you can't!' Ani said firmly. 'We have to free them!'

'We really don't,' he whispered.

'We really do,' she whispered back. 'Geez, Davenant. I would have thought you of all people would know what it's like to be stuck somewhere you don't want to live.'

Will stifled a gasp. That was a low, low blow.

But a very, very effective one.

'Please, Master William,' Juliet implored again. 'It is our destiny to be free.'

'It is everyone's destiny to be free,' Lady Macbeth corrected. 'Unless they need to be murdered.'

'Or they're already dead,' Yorick moaned.

Will could feel all the eyes, big, small and non-existent on him. He didn't have the time. He didn't have the bandwidth. He didn't have a story.

And he also knew, he didn't have a choice.

'All right,' he sighed, to an eruption of cheers from his new friends. 'I'll do it.'

'Excellent,' said Ani, peering down at the book intently. 'So how do we do this, can we just—'

She picked up Yorick's skull and tried to prise him from the page.

'OI!' he yelled, sticking to the page with the word glue that bound them all. 'What are you doing?! You trying to kill me?! Again?!'

'Sorry,' Ani grimaced, putting him back. 'My bad. So what do you need to do?'

'Tell my story,' Will shrugged. 'Whatever that means. I don't have a story to tell.'

'With our support, you cannot fail!' Puck exclaimed, taking flight. 'So let us help you find your tale!'

Puck floated down and touched Yorick on his skull, transforming him into a skeletal piglet with a curly tail.

'Seriously?' the skull moaned, before letting out a gentle *oink*.

'We are sworn to the Bard's service, we will help him with whatever he needs,' Lady Macbeth continued. 'Guidance. Advice. Weaponry . . .'

'And all our friends are always happy to help too,' Juliet added enthusiastically.

'Your friends?' Will asked. 'What . . . like, the other characters from the book? The ones on the outside?'

'Even them,' Lady Macbeth nodded.

'But . . . how?' Ani asked. 'You said you were trapped?'

'We are – and life could be much better,' said Puck, flying up as far as his words would stretch. 'Until then, we can send a letter.'

'A letter?' Will queried. 'I mean, no offence, but it's not like you can just nip down the post office.'

'No, Master Will,' Juliet giggled, gently raising her hands. 'Not your letters. *Ours.*'

At her command, individual letters from the words began to lift from the page, forming golden sentences all around the room – *Juliet 4 Romeo, can you bring milk, out of loo paper, are you dead yet?*

'So long as the book is open, we can communicate with our associates in the outside world,' Lady Macbeth explained.

'That's so cool,' Ani gasped as the letters floated out of the open window. 'So you'll help him? Will – the Bard – with anything?'

'Anything he wants,' said Juliet earnestly. 'Although we will only act for good. We're not going to hurt anyone, are we? Are. We?'

She looked pointedly at Lady Macbeth.

'I only make the suggestions,' Lady M shrugged. 'Not my fault what people do with them.'

'Then help him with this!' Ani said excitedly. 'Will wants to save Arden Heights.'

The Shakespeareans gasped.

'Arden Heights is in danger?' Juliet stammered.

'It is,' Ani confirmed. 'The flats might be sold to a developer – Egeus wants to take our home and . . .'

The rest of her sentence was drowned out by outraged exclamations from the Shakespeareans.

'This wicked plan is truly rotten,' sulked Puck, summoning up a black cloud to hang over the book. 'These villains must talk out their—'

'Boneheads,' said Yorick, shaking his skull.

Lady Macbeth carefully considered the predicament.

'Who do we kill first?' she asked eventually.

'Say it isn't so?' Juliet nearly wept. 'This place is . . . magical.'

'It really is,' Ani agreed. 'Which is why Will wants to stop them. *Don't you*, Will?'

It wasn't a question so much as a command.

'I do,' Will said cautiously. 'But I don't think these

guys . . .'

'We will be your advisors and friends,' Juliet swore.

'With a touch of magic, so things aren't tragic,' Puck winked, blowing them a kiss made of stars.

'*Oink, oink, oink,*' Yorick moaned.

'I still say just start murdering people,' Lady Macbeth suggested with a dismissive shrug.

'OK, so,' Ani began, 'here's the sitch . . .'

'IT WAS YOU, WASN'T IT?!' a man's voice bellowed outside Will's bedroom door.

'Are these the evil usurpers, coming to claim your castle?' Lady M asked, yanking a dagger from her skirts. 'Be not afeared. I've got this.'

'Shhhh!' Will said. 'My mum will hear you.'

'Wait,' said Ani, pushing an airborne Puck back down into the book. 'That's Ben!'

'Well, I figured since it was OK for you to park in my space, it was OK for me to use yours for a little storage!' Mary shouted.

'A little storage!' Ben roared. 'You filled my parking space with about fifty years of *National Geographic* magazine!'

'At least you'll have some light reading material until you MOVE YOUR CAR!'

'I have met pig-headed mules less stubborn than you!' Ben yelled.

'Really?' Mary shot back. 'You must introduce me to your family some time.'

'Just . . . just stay out of my space!'

'Stay out of my flat!'

'Stay out of my face!'

'With pleasure!' Mary roared. 'And I can see the family resemblance!'

Will heard the front door slam and his mother let out a scream of frustration.

'Wow,' Will whistled, shaking his head.

'Geez,' Ani echoed.

'I know,' Juliet sighed, clutching her hands to her heart. 'Isn't it wonderful? They're in love!'

'WHAT?!' Will cried. 'Did you not just hear that?'

'Told you,' said Ani with a smile, offering the young heroine a dinky high five. 'I'm with Jools.'

'You've been holding your breath underwater too long,' Will scoffed. 'They can't stand each other.'

'Two things you must understand about love,' Lady Macbeth said. 'Firstly, the path never runs smoothly.'

'That's true,' Ani agreed. 'Ben's had some seriously weird dates. This one woman would only eat food that began with a G. Another tried to cleanse his aura with some daffodils from the petrol station.'

'Secondly,' Lady Macbeth continued, 'it will probably kill you. Or you'll kill each other.'

'Good to know,' Will said, as Ani giggled and offered Lady Macbeth her own high five.

'Like B and B, a feisty pair,' Puck offered with a wink, transforming Yorick back to his morose self. 'Forsooth, I feel love in the air.'

'Who and what now?' Will asked.

'Beatrice and Benedick – oh, it's just the loveliest story!' Juliet said, dancing around the page with her hands clutched to her heart. 'They were sworn enemies, never had a kind word to say . . . until their friends told each of them that they were madly in love with each other. And then they decided that they were!'

'They're dead now,' Yorick groaned.

'No, they are not, you knave!' Juliet tinkled, giving Yorick a dink on his skull. 'They're running a highly successful couples' therapy practice.'

'So,' Will began, 'their friends . . . tricked them?'

'Isn't it romantic?' Juliet sighed.

'Not really, no,' Will said. 'In fact . . . that's messed up.'

'No, no, Master William,' Juliet insisted. 'Don't you see? All their friends did was make them realize what they really felt! You can't make someone do what they don't want to.'

'Amen,' muttered Lady Macbeth.

'I'm telling you!' Juliet insisted. 'Where there is that much passion, there is so much love waiting to happen . . .'

'Or a murder trial,' Lady Macbeth shrugged. 'But both are entertaining in their own ways.'

'. . . they just need to realize it,' Juliet said with a smile.

Will considered this. Out of love or murder, he definitely knew which one he thought was more likely.

'I hear you, J,' Ani echoed. 'But, listen, we've got to shoot, we need to get on the case.'

'Leave the pages, let us roam!' Puck cried, flying from the book. 'We can help you save your home.'

'No,' said Will firmly, moving over towards the book. 'No, no, no, no, no. Thank you for the offer, but this is complicated enough.'

'Forsooth, young William!' Juliet said in a panic. 'Stay your hand! You have our sworn oath that we can—'

She was silenced by the decisive sound of a book being shut.

'Riiiiiiiggggghhhht,' said Ani, as the golden words dissolved before her eyes. 'So you kept that quiet.'

'I only just found out myself,' Will grimaced. 'And you cannot tell anyone! People think I'm enough of a freak as it is.'

'Who says you're a freak?' Ani asked. 'I mean, you're a bit weird and dress like you're doing an Arctic trek every day. But who doesn't have their quirks? Aren't we all freaks? Who's told you that?'

'Just . . . people,' Will muttered.

'Well, they're wrong,' Ani said decisively. 'And we will find a way to free your friends. But for now, we need to get moving. You ready?'

As Ani strode out of the room, Will realized that once again, it wasn't really a question.

And as for his answer?

He honestly had no idea.

CHAPTER VII

The Taming of the Shrewd

'OK,' said Ani, the moment they reached the lift. 'We'll work from the bottom of the building to the top. First stop, flat 1 – Ms Minola. Let's start with the hardest and work backwards.'

Will didn't relish the thought of spending time with the grumpy lady from the previous night. She'd seemed pretty angry and he suspected they would have a fight on their hands. And Will didn't know how to put up a fight.

'All right,' he said, pulling his jumper collar against the already growing heat of the morning as the lift reached the bottom floor. 'What's the plan here?'

'We're just going to politely ask her to reconsider her position using reason and persuasion,' she declared as they reached the door of flat 1. In a block of identical flats, many of the residents had chosen to adorn their front doors with ornate handles, or fancy numbers. But not Ms Minola. Will suspected her door had been there, totally unchanged, as long as his grandmother's potpourri.

'Here we go,' said Ani confidently.

She plastered on a big smile and knocked briskly at the door three times. Will felt a flutter of nerves in his belly. He wasn't used to doing things like this – he preferred to stay in the background. It was safer that way. This felt uncomfortable. Awkward. Embarrassing.

He was considering making a run for it when he heard shuffling footsteps approaching the other side of the door. Ani grinned at him as an orchestra of clunks and clanks signalled a lot of security chains being undone.

'What?' came the abrupt enquiry when the door opened a crack, revealing one side of its owner's ferocious face.

'Uh, good morning, Ms Minola,' Ani said politely, holding up one of her flyers. 'We were hoping we could talk to you about the proposed purchase by Egeus. We have some serious concerns about the nature of—'

'Not interested,' the old lady snapped and slammed the door shut again. Ani looked confused.

'Oh, well, we tried,' said Will, starting gratefully back towards the lift. 'Perhaps this isn't such a—'

He was interrupted by the sound of three more, rather louder, knocks echoing down the hallway. Will closed his eyes and groaned. This was not going to go well. He turned back to flat 1, just as the door opened again.

'I already told you, I'm not interested!' Ms Minola barked at Ani, who stood her ground with a now rather strained smile.

'I understand that you are a busy person,' Ani said through her teeth, 'but this is an important decision, affecting so many vulnerable people and I just want to ensure you are in full possession of the facts before you—'

'Are you completely stupid, or just profoundly irritating?' Ms Minola snapped. 'For the last time, I don't want to hear what you or anyone has to say – so why don't you just go away and leave me to my day in peace!'

The door slammed in Ani's face again. Hard.

'Come on,' said Will, tugging at his companion's elbow. 'It's not going to happen, let's just give up.'

'Give up?' said Ani, her eyes aflame. Will could practically see her temperature rising. 'Give up on all these people? On their home? If you – or her – think I'm just going to walk away from this, you've got another—'

Before she could finish her own tirade, Ani hammered on Ms Minola's door for a third time.

'Right,' she yelled through the door, making Will wince. 'You might not care, but there are lots of us here who do! If Egeus buys this building, dozens of elderly people will be forced out of their homes against their will into uncertain futures – and with not nearly enough money to stay in the area many have lived all their lives! And if you can't even make time to listen to a considered argument about how we all need to stand together against this greedy attempt to steal our flats, then you're nothing more than, than, than . . . a selfish old bat!'

The words rang through the empty corridor like shots from a gun.

'Reason and persuasion, you say,' Will whispered to the irate Ani.

'URGH!' she replied, throwing up her arms and storming back towards the lift, jabbing the button like she was stabbing it with a dagger.

Before the lift could arrive, however, the sound of multiple latches being undone filled the hallway again. Ani was still fuming, her arms folded angrily across her T-shirt. But Will turned around, caught between terror and intrigue to see what Ms Minola would do in response to Ani's outburst. Would she shout? Tell their parents? Cast a spell?

So he was surprised to see the formidable woman standing in her doorway with a curious smile.

'Well, why didn't you say so?' she called down the hallway. 'I suppose you'd better come in.'

Will knew that all the flats in Arden Heights must be identical. But it hadn't occurred to him that, depending on which side of the building they were, they would be arranged differently. So when he stepped into Ms Minola's flat, on the opposite side of the building to Rex's, it threw him. It was the same as his flat, but the other way around. So whereas Rex's bathroom was on the left as you walked in, Ms Minola's was on the right. Rex's kitchen was on the right, so hers was on the other side. It was slightly odd at first to be in a mirror image of his present residence – but very quickly his attention was drawn by something else.

'Wow,' said Ani, echoing the more polite end of Will's thoughts. 'What's all this?'

Will was used to seeing a flat full of paperwork – he and Mum were still wading through his grandfather's memoirs after all. But in Ms Minola's flat, the papers weren't in neat bundles on the floor. They were plastered all over the walls, over doors, even inside the bathroom. There were newspaper articles, photographs, handwritten notes joined by pieces of string . . . It reminded Will of the kind of shows Mum liked to watch. The kind, worryingly, where someone had committed a horrible crime that needed to be solved. It would make a fantastic drawing, though . . .

'Drink?' Ms Minola asked ferociously, apparently unaware of just how bizarre her surroundings were. 'I think I have some lemonade somewhere.'

'Thanks,' said Ani absently, walking over to the wall to read some of the papers as Ms Minola hobbled into her kitchen.

'Erm, did you tell Ben we were coming here?' Will whispered to Ani. If some massive crime had been – or was about to be – committed, he didn't want to end up on Ms Minola's wall.

'Yes, yes, yes,' said Ani dismissively, squinting at a diagram with a woman's name in the centre. 'He made me write a list of everyone to make sure they were OK before he'd let me come out, he's such a nerd. Who is . . . Bianca?'

'Maybe it's her?' Will suggested. 'Does anyone know her first name?'

'Bianca is my daughter,' Ms Minola said, having appeared like a ghost behind them.

Will nearly jumped out of his skin.

'Where is she?' Ani asked with her customary bluntness.

'I . . . I don't know,' Ms Minola said more gently. 'I've

been trying to find her. For many years now . . .'

'I'm . . . we're sorry,' said Will, accepting his glass of lemonade. 'We didn't mean to pry.'

'It's not prying if it's right there in front of you,' Ms Minola said plainly. 'Come on through.'

They walked into her front room – again, the inversion of Will's – and she ushered them on to the threadbare brown sofa.

'So,' she said agreeably. 'What is it you've come here to say?'

'Oh, right, OK,' said Ani, pulling a flyer off her clipboard. 'So, Ben and I – he's a lawyer – have looked at this Egeus deal and we don't think it's right. If people want to sell their flats, then good luck to them. But to force out people who call Arden Heights home . . . it's not fair.'

Ms Minola considered this.

'That's a good point,' she said, sipping her cup of tea with a nod.

Ani's face brightened like the sunny day outside.

'Does that mean you'll vote against the development?' she said eagerly.

Ms Minola took another sip of her tea.

'No,' she said quietly.

Will recognized the tired face of a woman who'd had a difficult journey through life. His mum's face often looked the same. Ms Minola had bigger problems than

Arden Heights. He gestured to Ani that it was time to go.

'Why not?' Ani replied.

Will shot Ani a look that told her she was out of line. Ms Minola put her tea on the table with a small smile.

'Because leaving this place feels like the best thing I could do,' she said. 'I need to get away. From here. From Bianca. From everything.'

She said it with the kind of sadness that had been hardened by the years. Will's grief was still so molten – he couldn't trust that it wouldn't burst out of him at any moment. But Ms Minola's pain was like rock – hard, immovable, cold. He nodded empathetically. Ms Minola clearly didn't want to talk about this.

'What happened?' Ani barged in. 'Did you and Bianca have a fight?'

'I wish,' snorted Ms Minola.

Once again, Will understood that this was a situation that was obviously very delicate and difficult for their host. And once again, Ani clearly did not.

'I don't understand,' she said, her nose wrinkled. 'So if you haven't had a fight, what's the problem?'

Will waited for Ms Minola to tell Ani to mind her own business, or to ask them to leave, or simply to shout at them. But instead, she tilted her head and looked at Ani sideways.

'You like to say things as they are, don't you?' she said.

Ani shrugged. 'Is there a better way?' she said.

Ms Minola smiled again. 'No,' she replied. 'I'm not sure there is.'

She carefully replaced her tea on the coaster and took a steadying breath.

'I haven't had a fight with Bianca,' she began slowly. 'In fact, I've never met Bianca. Well, only once.'

'What?' said Ani, without waiting for Ms Minola to finish. 'How . . . I don't understand. You're her mum . . .'

Ani trailed off. Perhaps she'd finally realized how rude she was being, Will wasn't sure. But Ms Minola just looked out across her view of the gardens.

'There was a time – and I very much hope it is behind us now – where it was felt that a woman who wasn't married, who didn't have a partner, wasn't able to raise a child by herself,' Ms Minola said.

Will closed his eyes and hoped that Ani's next response would be gentler.

'Why?' she asked softly, to his great relief.

Ms Minola looked deep into Ani's eyes.

'Child,' she began. 'No one has ever adequately answered that question.'

Will looked at Ani's face, twisted in confusion. He waited for her direct response. But this time, she said nothing.

'And so, as so many have before and since, I fell in

love and had a baby,' Ms Minola said with a proud smile. 'She was beautiful and perfect and I named her Bianca. I loved her the moment I saw her. There is no love that competes with a mother's for her child, it's . . .'

Will felt Ani fidget on the sofa next to him. He nudged her to sit still.

'It is everything,' Ms Minola concluded. 'And she was everything to me. And then . . .'

Ms Minola trailed off. Will knew she needed to find her own words in her own time. And this time, so did Ani.

'And then,' Ms Minola said with a broken voice. 'They took her.'

'Who?' Ani practically whispered. 'Who took your baby?'

Ms Minola let out a snort.

'The doctors. My parents. Our vicar,' she said. 'They told me I wasn't fit to raise my own child. That she'd be better off with someone else. That I was no good for her on my own. That I couldn't give her a good life. And, to my everlasting regret, I listened.'

'That's awful,' said Ani, echoing Will's own thoughts.

'It was,' Ms Minola practically whispered. 'It really was. I was utterly heartbroken. So I threw myself into my career – I used to be an actress, you see. I travelled the world, played all the great roles, won all the acclaim . . .'

'Oh, wow. My mum's an actress too!' Ani said enthusiastically as Ms Minola pulled out a picture of her younger self onstage to show them. 'She's going to be in a musical in New York later this year.'

Will stopped the question on his tongue, now wasn't the time.

'Tell her to enjoy it while it lasts,' said Ms Minola bitterly. 'Acting, like life itself, doesn't have good roles for older women. Both favour the young. I tried to hide from the pain. But it always found me. When someone takes your child, they don't just take your baby. They take your motherhood. I never got to brush her hair. To put her to bed. To nurse her when she was sick. To cook her a meal. They stole all that from me. I just pray that someone else was able to give them to her.'

'Do you know where she went?' Ani asked, putting the aged photograph back on the coffee table. 'Bianca, I mean?'

Ms Minola pointed to the labyrinth of papers all around her house.

'That's what I've been trying to find out,' she said. 'Bianca will be fifty this Friday. I promised myself that if I hadn't found her by then, I would give up the search.'

'Why?' Will found himself asking before he'd had time to think if he should.

Ms Minola raised her sad eyes to his.

'Because it's becoming clearer with every year that passes, that Bianca doesn't want to be found.'

The words hung heavily in the air. Will didn't know what to say. That was such a sad story.

'But . . . how do you know she doesn't want to be found?' Ani said, her nose wrinkling up. 'I mean, you can't know that until you ask her yourself?'

'When you give a baby up – whether you want to or not – the rule is that they must want you to find them,' Ms Minola explained. 'If Bianca was looking for me, she would have been able to find me, I left my details in all the right places. And she hasn't. Nothing.'

'OK,' said Ani, her voice rising with what Will already knew was her brewing an idea. 'But what if she doesn't know you want to find her? I mean – no offence or anything – but if she thinks you didn't want her . . .'

This time it was Ani's voice that trailed away.

'All I'm saying,' she gulped, 'is that perhaps these "places" aren't the best way. Maybe you need to reach out to her more directly? Let her know you're there?'

'And how would I do that?' Ms Minola asked curiously.

'I dunno,' Ani shrugged. 'She's probably on social media – I mean, everyone is. Have you tried that?'

'Er, Ani?' Will said, a growing sense of discomfort rising in his chest. 'We don't know about this stuff, perhaps we'd better get back to saving Arden Heights.'

'This is to save Arden Heights!' Ani said brightly. 'If Ms Minola found Bianca, maybe she'd want to stay? Wouldn't you?'

Ms Minola looked around the room covered in investigations for her lost daughter.

'Maybe,' she smiled.

'Right, then!' said Ani, pulling out her phone. 'Let's get you set up. Do you have a computer?'

Ms Minola pointed to the ancient laptop on her ancient desk.

'Great!' said Ani, sitting down at it and tapping away at the keys. 'I created my account myself so that I can speak to my mum, I think I remember how to do it.'

'Um, I don't think this is a good idea,' Will said quietly. 'Anyone can put anything on social media.'

'Including Bianca,' said Ani firmly, not taking her eyes from the screen.

'Do you really think so?' Ms Minola said, unmissable hope in her voice.

'I really do,' said Ani confidently, taking a photo of Ms Minola and another of the picture of her younger self before uploading both. Will felt weird about all this. But he'd already said something – what more could he do?

'Right, there you are, easy as that!' Ani declared with a flourish. 'You're now online. All we have to do is write a post about Bianca and ask people to share it. So give me some details – you said she's fifty this week, that's a great start, so her birthdate is . . .'

Will watched uncomfortably as Ani detailed Bianca and Ms Minola's personal information, ready to share it with the world. He understood that Ani's heart was in the right place. But he couldn't shake the feeling it was leading Ms Minola in the wrong direction.

'And then we ask people to share the post. I'll start – and make sure people can message you directly if they know anything. There!' Ani declared, hitting the return key with a flourish. 'It's done! I've got a good feeling about this.'

'You do?' said Ms Minola.

'I don't,' said Will quietly, earning him a hard nudge from Ani.

'Well, I do,' Ani declared, standing up with a grin. 'Listen, Ms Minola, keep us posted and I'll let you know if I hear anything, OK? But will you please have a think about the vote? It would mean so much to us.'

She held out her flyer again with a pleading smile. And this time, Ms Minola accepted both.

'You're a force of nature, young lady,' she said, not unkindly. 'You remind me of a younger me.'

'Well, remind yourself of a younger you,' said Ani, standing up to leave. 'Because, Ms Minola, you seem pretty awesome to me.'

The older lady chuckled softly.

'That's very kind of you to say,' she said. 'Now be on your way, you young scamps. I'm sure you have other residents to pester.'

'We certainly do,' Ani agreed with a beaming smile. 'Hang on in there, Ms Minola. Like I say, I've got a good feeling about this.'

They walked back through Ms Minola's crime scene of a flat and into the hallway.

'Well, that couldn't have gone much better!' Ani erupted in an excited whisper the moment the door was latched behind them. 'I think she's going to change her mind! Right – next one! I'm on a roll!'

Will followed his excited friend as she skipped towards the lift. Ani was on a roll, all right.

He just worried about who she might flatten in her path.

CHAPTER VIII

Stairlift-Crossed Lovers

'So, who's next?' Will asked, as Ani consulted her list.

'Flat 11,' she informed him. 'Monty.'

'Is he grumpy too?' Will asked. Ms Minola had certainly softened during their visit, but he wasn't sure he had the energy for another angry neighbour.

'Nah, Monty's chill,' Ani said with a wave of her hand. 'But I'm surprised we need to have this conversation – I thought he loved living at Arden Heights, especially with Sylvie here. I would have thought he'd be a loud vote against . . . Oh, rats, I hit the wrong floor, we're back on two.'

The lift pinged and the doors opened to reveal Angela and Julian chatting happily on the second floor.

'Oh, hello, little ones!' Angela said, a little too loudly as they stepped into the lift. 'What are you up to today?

Not causing mischief, I hope?'

She sounded like she was both joking and not.

'No,' said Ani with a falsely sweet smile, pulling her clipboard to her chest. 'Just . . . a little project.'

'Well, good for you!' said Julian warmly, before returning to poking at his phone. 'Now why won't this text message send?'

'Hold on,' said Ani, taking it gently from his hands. 'No – you're recording a voice note. You need to press that one, there.'

She pointed to the screen and handed it back to the kindly gentleman.

'Oh, I am such a fool!' Julian beamed. 'When the age is in, the wit is out! Thank you, dear Ani. I keep sending my daughter pictures of the inside of my pocket, I've no idea how to work this thing.'

He shoved the phone in his jacket and picked up a cash tin from the ground.

'So, what are you doing today?' Ani asked, pressing the button for the first floor.

'We're on committee business,' said Julian proudly. 'We need to bank these subscription funds today, there's a lot of money in here. And if we happen to go for a nice lunch afterwards . . . Oh, I'm a clot! I've left my wallet upstairs. Angela, we'll just need to nip back to my flat or I'll be washing dishes in the cafe!'

'Oh, no need!' said Angela. 'Just take it out of the tin – you can pay it back afterwards. After all, I know where you live!'

She laughed brightly. But once again, it didn't entirely sound like a joke. Julian looked uncertainly at the tin.

'I don't know,' he said. 'I'd rather not. I'd worry about paying it back, I'm so forgetful these days, I'd lose my head if it wasn't screwed on!'

'Well, then, I'll remind you,' said Angela, putting a firm hand on his arm. 'Come on, you know what the queue will be like at the post office and it closes soon. We're on our way now – don't make us late.'

It was said with a smile. But it was clearly an order.

'Well, all right, then,' said Julian reluctantly. 'If you're sure.'

'I am,' said Angela as the lift pinged at the first floor. 'See you later, children – keep those little noses clean!'

She smiled at them as they left the lift, and yet it wasn't really a smile at all. Will couldn't put his finger on what it was that bothered him about Angela . . .

'She's so creepy,' Ani stated, expressing it perfectly. 'She's like deadly nightshade. Looks all right, but just might poison you.'

'She really is,' Will agreed as they walked down the corridor. 'So . . . Monty?'

'He's Italian, he's a widower and has two grown-up

daughters, Georgia and Regina,' Ani informed him. 'He's a really sweet guy. I'm sure I can make him see sense.'

'By "seeing sense", you mean "agree with you",' Will pointed out. Ani's nose wrinkled again.

'Of course,' she said, shrugging her shoulders. 'They're the same thing.'

Will waited for Ani to smile and show that she was joking.

She wasn't.

Will struggled to keep up with Ani's brisk pace down the corridor.

'Oi!' yelled Caleb, emerging from a cleaning cupboard like a monster on a ghost train. 'No running in the corridors! Someone's gonna get hurt!'

'Yep, sure they are, Caleb!' Ani shouted behind them as she powered on.

'He's only trying to do his job,' Will pointed out.

'He's only trying to be a pain in the— Uh-oh,' Ani grinned as they were hit by an overwhelming food smell. 'Is that . . .'

'Victoria sponge,' Will confirmed as they turned the corner to find Rosie from the gardening committee standing at the doorway to flat 14, holding a massive cake on a silver platter.

'It just seemed a shame for it to go to waste,' Rosie giggled.

'Er, thank you, Rosie,' Patrick replied. 'Although I still haven't finished yesterday's . . .'

'Well, let me help you,' said Rosie, wedging herself in the door.

'Uh . . . now's not the best time, actually,' said Patrick awkwardly. 'You see, I'm . . .'

'Hello, Rosie,' said Hemie stiffly, appearing behind her host with a slice of cake on a plate. 'I just popped round to practise our quickstep for the tea dance. Over a slice of my famous mango lassi cake.'

'Daaaannng,' Ani exhaled slowly. 'I think Hemie just declared war. Pulling out the mango lassi *and* a quick-step. Power move.'

'Murder on the dance floor?' Will suggested, making Ani stifle a giggle.

'I see,' said Rosie, her mouth puckered like a grumpy belly button. 'I was under the impression that Patrick preferred the foxtrot and a Victoria sponge. He likes something a little more . . . refined and classic.'

'They're both very lovely,' Patrick tried to interject unsuccessfully.

'I'm afraid you're mistaken,' said Hemie icily. 'Patrick likes something fruitier with a little more spring in its step.'

'He ate my Victoria sponge first!' Rosie insisted.

'Well, now he wants my mango lassi cake!' Hemie snapped back.

'Ladies, please!' Patrick said calmly. 'You're both . . . very talented bakers.'

'But you can only have one favourite,' Rosie insisted, pushing her Victoria sponge under his nose.

'Yes, Patrick!' Hemie agreed, taking a huge forkful of her mango lassi and holding it to his lips. 'Whose cake do you want?'

As Will and Ani struggled to contain their laughter, another door opened along the hallway.

'Oh, hello, everyone – you all right?' said Antoine pleasantly, carrying a bin bag.

'Antoine, hello,' said Patrick, smiling gratefully. 'Good to see you.'

'You too, Patrick,' said Antoine, clearing his throat. 'Oooh, are we having cake? Smashing.'

'There's not enough to go around,' said Rosie curtly, clutching her gigantic cake and not taking her eyes off Patrick.

Hemie archly eyed her neighbour up and down.

'Looks like there's plenty to me,' she said.

'Why, you . . .' Rosie began to rage.

'Er, hi, everyone,' said Ani, emerging from their hiding place and brandishing a flier. 'We were wondering if we could speak to you about the Egeus development? Your votes are crucial to ensure the survival of this warm and vibrant community and—'

'I can't get out of this place fast enough!' Rosie declared, starting to storm off down the corridor. 'It'll be refreshing to find a better class of neighbour!'

'Me too!' said Hemie, grabbing her handbag and storming off in the opposite direction. 'Although if you want to leave your Victoria sponge, those developers will be needing some cement!'

Will and Ani stood awkwardly. Patrick and Antoine stood awkwardly.

'So, er, about the development?' Ani said quietly. 'Can we count on your vote against?'

Antoine and Patrick looked sadly at one another.

'I think it might be time to move on,' Patrick said eventually. 'Best for everyone.'

'Of course,' Antoine barely whispered. 'For the best.'

The two men smiled their farewells, Patrick closing his door and Antoine shuffling off with his bin bag and a woeful smile.

'I think your roll just stopped,' said Will.

'We're not giving up,' said Ani determinedly, striding down the hallway to flat 11, where she briskly knocked on the door.

Unlike Ms Minola's flat, the door to Monty's had clearly had some love and care, a floral number 11 in its centre and a large welcome mat at the base. Two large vine plants sat outside the door, their leaves intertwining as they rose up. This flat's entrance was very inviting – Will hoped that its owner would be the same.

It was only moments before they heard soft footsteps rushing towards the door and there were no latches unbolted this time. The door opened straight away, to reveal Monty's smiling face.

'*Bambini!*' he cried with a grin. 'It is good to see you, come in, come in!'

They were ushered inside with no question about why they were there. Again, Will found himself in an identical flat to his own, this one orientated the same way as his. But again, the inside was completely different. Whereas his grandfather's was dark and scholarly, Ms Minola's bare and practical, Monty's flat wouldn't have looked out of place in a holiday brochure. With the sun shining in through the curtainless windows, across the tiled floor and terracotta walls, Will felt like he was abroad – or at least what he imagined that would be like, he'd never actually left the country. There were plants and flowers everywhere – it was a riot of colour and joy. Now this would make a happy picture. It was a home that had known love.

Monty directed them through to his front room, where the massive French windows were open to the fresh sea air and stunning view. A small table sat on the balcony, which was also bursting with the colour of countless flowers. It was really beautiful. Will reflected that Rex's flat could use some of this love and care.

'Please, please, you sit!' said Monty, whose every enthusiastic word was accompanied by equally enthusiastic hand gestures. 'Ah, I know what you need! Panettone! I bought a new one yesterday. It's never too early for a panettone! Growing children must eat, yes!'

'Thanks, Monty, but we just . . .' Ani began in vain. Monty was already scampering off to his kitchen, singing to himself as he went. Although he was older than Ms Minola – quite a lot older, Will guessed – Monty moved with an energy of a younger man. Whereas Ms M seemed weighed down by life, Monty seemed to feed off it, his eyes dancing and his steps spritely. It was infectious – and as he returned with a song on his lips and a huge cake on a tray, Will couldn't help but smile at both. He pulled at his jumper against the heat. Monty's balcony was pretty. But, wow, was it hot . . .

'Just take it off,' Ani said, looking at him curiously. 'You're wearing a T-shirt underneath. You must be boiling.'

'Nah,' Will lied as Monty stepped back out on the balcony. 'Don't really feel the heat.'

Their host put the panettone – a big, chocolatey,

cakey bread thing – in the centre of the table before cutting three big slices on to plates and handing them out with a glass of juice.

'*Prego!*' he said with a satisfied smile, gesturing keenly to their plates. 'Eat! Drink! Children need hearts and bellies full of joy! And not-children need them too!'

He raised his glass, before tucking into his panettone with gusto. Will took a bite of his. It was delicious. He had to say this much for Arden Heights – he wasn't going to go hungry here.

'*Bellissimo!*' Monty declared with a chef's kiss. 'Now, *bambini*, why you come see old Monty? What can I do for you?'

Will couldn't help but contrast Monty's openness with Ms Minola's suspicion. He was a virtual stranger to this man, yet he'd welcomed him into his home like a friend. It was a nice way to be.

'Well,' said Ani through a mouth of crumbs, 'I'm hoping I can persuade you not to sell your flat to Egeus, Monty. We just wanted to talk to you about it. You're such a big part of the community here – we could really use you and your vote.'

'Ah,' said Monty, his face falling a little for the first time. 'I understand, *bambina*. And you're right, I do not want to go.'

Ani sat up like a meerkat.

'Great!' she said. 'So vote against! If twenty of us oppose it, Egeus can't take our homes, we'd be—'

Monty held up a hand against the volley of words coming his way.

'I wish it were that simple, little one,' he said. 'If it were up to me, I know what my heart would do. But there are other hearts for me to consider.'

'Your daughters?' Ani concluded.

'*Sì*,' Monty confirmed with a heavy nod. 'My girls love their papa, they want what's best for me.'

'Well, surely that's staying here, isn't it?' Ani insisted with a frown. 'In your home. With your friends.'

'Age is a funny thing, *bambina*,' Monty said with a sad smile. 'When my beloved Maria – may she rest with the angels – gave me two daughters, I vowed that I would care for them until my dying breath. But as that day approaches, it is them who must now care for me.'

'What do they want?' Will asked, still a little confused.

'What every parent dreams of!' Monty said, throwing his hands to the heavens. 'To take care of their papa! They want me to come and live with them! The money from the flat will buy an extension to Georgia's house; Regina lives nearby and they want me with them for when the day comes – and that day may not be long – when I will need their help.'

'But that day's not today,' Ani said firmly. 'I don't

know anyone more full of life than you, Monty. It could be years before you need that kind of support.'

The old man's face lit up like the sunrise.

'*Grazie, bambina,*' he said with a small bow. Will had to give it to Ani – her direct nature might have its rougher edges. But her honesty clearly meant a lot to this kind and joyful gentlemen.

'But I also think they are right,' he said, the smile erased by a weary sigh. 'Besides, I have other reasons to leave this place behind.'

Ani leant forward and softened her voice.

'Are there too many memories of Maria here?' she almost whispered. Monty smiled. He turned and blew a kiss to what Will assumed must be a photograph of his late wife on the living room wall.

'This is a reason to stay, not to leave,' he said. 'Maria and I had many happy years at Arden Heights. This place breathes with her memories. I love this.'

'Why, then?' Ani asked, the familiar wrinkle returning to her nose.

'*Santa Maria!* For the only reason anyone should do anything!' Monty shouted, raising his hands up dramatically.

'Money?' Will guessed.

'You're ill?' Ani tried, tactlessly.

'No, *bambini*, no!' Monty laughed. These are not

reasons for living! There is only one, and it is the greatest of all! It is *AMORE*!'

The unfamiliar word rang around the balcony, reverberating around the flowerpots and out into the ocean beyond.

'You what?' Ani asked, her nose now practically in her eyebrows.

Monty threw his head back with a joyful laugh.

'Ah, my young friends, you have so much to learn!' he cried, standing up so suddenly, he sent his chair clattering across the balcony. 'I'm talking about LOVE! *Bambini*, I'M IN LOVE!'

Will shot up to collect Monty's chair, just in time to stop their host from landing on the floor.

'I knew it – Sylvie from flat 34,' Ani said brightly. 'She's so lovely! When Ben and I moved down here, she brought us some of her jam!'

'Ah, her jam!' declared Monty, clasping his heart. 'Is like angel song in a gingham jar.'

'She's single too,' Ani continued, 'and I've definitely picked up on vibes between you. What's stopping you?'

Monty took the first breath Will had observed him taking.

'My girls,' he sighed. 'They say I am an old fool. That it would be to dishonour their mother. That I need to move away and forget about Sylvie. And I think they're probably right.'

'No, they're not!' Ani declared, thumping the table.

'Er, maybe they know what's best for their own dad,' Will said quietly.

'A happy life is what's best for their dad!' Ani proclaimed. 'Have you spoken to Sylvie yourself? Maybe it would sound better coming directly from you?'

'*Mamma mia*, no!' Monty exclaimed. 'Sylvie and I are good friends! I don't want to lose her.'

'You lose her if you move from Arden Heights,' Ani pointed out.

'Exactly!' said Monty, jumping up and sending the chair flying again. 'So you see, my friends, it is impossible! Better for Monty to accept his new life and be happy. And so I must leave.'

'Hmmmm,' said Ani, her mind whirring. 'I need to think about this.'

'That'll make a change,' Will muttered, not quietly enough if the stamp on his foot was anything to go by.

'It is impossible,' Monty repeated with a sad shake of his head.

Ani stood up and took the man's hand in hers.

'Nothing is impossible,' she said and clearly believed it. Will did not. He knew plenty about impossible situations. And he knew there were no solutions.

'We have to go,' said Ani, looking at her watch. 'But

will you promise me something, Monty?'

'For you, *bambina*, anything,' Monty said, placing his hand across his heart.

'Don't make a decision yet,' Ani pleaded. 'There has to be a way. And I'm going to find it.'

Monty's eyes crinkled in a thousand places. He took Ani's hand in his.

'*Grazie mille, bambina*,' he said softly. 'You have such spirit. Never take no for an answer! I had to ask my Maria to marry me five times before she agreed!'

'Well, she was right to say yes,' Ani beamed back at him. 'And I'm right about this. Hang in there, Monty. I'm on it. Come on, Will.'

She picked up her things and strode back through the flat. Will shook his head and looked back to Monty to thank him for his hospitality. The old man was smiling at him.

'My young friend, may I give you a piece of advice?' he said, leaning across the table.

'Sure,' Will shrugged.

'When a girl like that tells you to go somewhere,' Monty said, raising his glass. 'You'd be a fool not to follow. *Salute!*'

CHAPTER IX

Sigh No More

'Shall we go to yours?' Ani suggested as they closed the door to Monty's flat and headed back to the lift. 'Ben's got loads of work on and he's struggling to do it all and look after Olivia, but he won't let anyone else care for her.'

'Why's that?' Will asked.

'Olivia adopted him – he had a pretty rough childhood,' Ani explained. 'And now he's determined to care for her. But it's tough.'

This, Will understood. He thought about when his dad was really ill and his mum was trying to care for him and do her job. She was so tired all the time. And she'd still tried to make everything right for Will. He had no idea how she'd managed it. How anyone managed it.

'Fine,' he said as they headed back towards the lift.

'Although Mum won't be much better – Rex's place is still a tip and we've only got a few more days until we have to go back to my uncle's.'

'What's the deal with that?' Ani asked. 'Why do you guys have to live with him if he's such an idiot?'

'Money,' Will shrugged, pressing the lift button. 'We don't have any. He does.'

'How does that work?' Ani's wrinkled nose asked. 'He's your mum's brother, right? How come he's got money and your mum doesn't? They're family? Don't they share?'

'My uncle would tell you that he is sharing,' Will said darkly. 'But my parents really did share. They shared everything. Rent. Bills. Cooking. Housework. Their sandwiches . . .'

'Their sandwiches?' Ani laughed.

'My dad's hospital was near my mum's charity,' Will said. 'Every lunchtime they could, they'd meet up and share their sandwiches with each other. I used to think it was so cheesy.'

A wave of sadness drowned the happy memory. Will wished he could go back in time and turn all those moments over. He shouldn't have been embarrassed by how much his parents loved each other. He should have just basked in the warmth of it.

'Anyway,' he carried on, 'when Dad . . . when we lost

him, Mum tried to pay for everything herself. But—'

'You can't make half of something a whole,' Ani said quietly. 'I get it. But your mum will inherit half your grandad's money, right?' Ani continued.

'Wrong,' Will sighed as the lift arrived. 'My mum and Rex had a big fight years ago. He cut her out of his will. Everything goes to Claude. He told us.'

'Really?' said Ani, turning to look at him. 'I'm honestly surprised, that doesn't sound like the Rex I met. I mean, I didn't know the Duke well, but he always seemed pretty cool.'

'Yeah, well,' said Will quietly. 'I guess people aren't always how they seem.'

The lift doors opened and they were about to walk in, when Caleb stormed out carrying armfuls of cleaning products. They collided in the doorway, sending bottles and packets flying across the lift and hall.

'Now look what you've gone and done!' Caleb shouted at them. 'I told you! No running in the corridors! Someone's gonna get hurt!'

'All right, all right, keep your hair on,' Ani scoffed, picking up a bottle of polish. 'And we weren't running.'

'Sorry, Caleb,' Will muttered, grabbing two bottles of bleach and a dusting cloth. 'Here you go.'

'Hmmm,' said the caretaker, snatching the bottles from his hand. 'I'm watching you pair. Stay out of my way! Now clear off!'

'Gladly,' Ani called after him as Caleb stumbled off down the corridor. 'Well, there's someone who is exactly what they seem. A complete and utter–'

'You should cut him some slack,' said Will, watching the caretaker amble away. 'Sounds like he's had a hard life. My mum says that hurt people hurt people . . .'

Will trailed off. He knew for a fact his mum was wrong. But it was a nice theory. Mary was always kind and reasonable and–

'I SWEAR TO GOD IF I SEE ONE MORE RECEIPT FOR PAPER CLIPS I'M GOING TO RUN INTO THE SEA AND SWIM FOR THE NEAREST DESERT ISLAND!' he heard Mary explode inside the flat as they let themselves in.

'Er, maybe we should go to yours?' he said quickly.

'Sure,' said Ani, scurrying across the hallway and into his bedroom without invitation.

'Erm, what are you–' Will asked, but his question was answered when she emerged from his room holding the *Complete Works*.

'I figure we could use some advice,' she said. And Will didn't disagree.

They walked down the hall to Ani's flat, let themselves in through the unlocked door and headed straight for Ani's bedroom. In Ben's flat, Ani's room was the same as his, although she hadn't really made it her own either. It looked more like a guest room than a teenager's bedroom – not that Will really knew what one of those would be like.

'Well, that was a day,' said Ani, throwing herself on her bed. 'My head is like a beehive.'

'Mine too,' said Will, sitting on the floor next to her. 'What are we going to do?'

'No idea,' said Ani, handing the magical book to Will. 'But maybe six heads are better than one? Well, five heads and one skull.'

Will nodded. He took the book from Ani's hands and it immediately illuminated.

'That is so cool,' she said admiringly.

'Let's see,' he said more cautiously as he lifted the front cover again. At his touch, the golden words floated out of the book like dust being blown from a forgotten picture – and once again, as they swirled around Ani's bedroom, it wasn't long before they formed the solid shapes of his sworn Shakespearean protectors on top of the open pages. This time they were on an island, Juliet building a sandcastle, Puck swinging in a hammock, Yorick sipping from a cocktail with a straw . . . and Lady Macbeth throwing axes at a tree.

'Master William!' Juliet said with a happy curtsy. 'How farest thee on this fine day?'

'What are you plotting?' Lady Macbeth asked suspiciously. 'You both look like you have trouble in mind?'

'Trouble! Huzzah! My middle name!' Puck cried, taking flight and placing Yorick up a palm tree, before making bright pink hair sprout of his skull. 'So tell me, younglings, what's the game?'

'Hey!' Yorick groaned, his hollow eye sockets looking up at his new style. 'Can't a guy enjoy one last drink in peace?'

'Er, hi, everyone,' Will muttered, putting the book on the floor between him and Ani.

'Hello again!' Ani sang with an enthusiastic wave.

The characters variously waved back, nodded, or clanked their jawbones in salutation.

'Listen,' Ani began breathlessly, 'we need your advice. We've been to see Ms Minola, Monty and the gardening committee, and we need all of their support if we're going to save the Heights. But that's not going to be easy because . . .'

Will zoned out as Ani retold the stories of all the residents he'd met that day. Just in this one building, even a few flats, there was so much happening for everyone. He'd been so caught up in his own issues, it was easy to forget that everyone else had complicated lives too. Not that it made his any easier. He still had no idea what he was going to do about—

'Will!' Ani grumped a few minutes later. 'Are you even listening? We need to come up with a plan.'

'It seems to me,' said Juliet, thinking carefully, 'that all these poor souls wish to run away from Arden Heights because they have problems here. If we can solve the problems, their reasons for leaving will be gone.'

'Unless they all die,' sighed Yorick.

'A little magic, that's the ticket,' said Puck, whizzing around the page, stringing garlands of flowers across the palm trees. 'If you can't solve it, I can trick it.'

'I still vote murder,' said Lady Macbeth, raising her hand.

'We're not murdering anybody,' said Will calmly. 'But if anyone has any other suggestions?'

'Well,' Juliet began enthusiastically, 'I think Rosie should feign her own death so that Patrick will come mournfully to her tomb and then they'd be joyfully reunited forever.'

'Erm, on that,' said Will, scanning his poor knowledge of *Romeo and Juliet*, but pretty confident they all died at the end. 'Explain something to me. How does it . . . work? I mean you say that all the characters are free and doing stuff in the world. But aren't some of them . . .'

He tried not to look at Juliet.

'Dead?'

'Preach, friend,' Yorick mumbled.

Lady Macbeth shrugged.

'We are all but part way through our story,' she explained. 'We know not how it ends. Any more than you know the end of yours.'

That made some sense. Although he still had no idea how he was supposed to free these characters. Will didn't have a story. At least, not one he wanted to tell.

'Will poor Monty have to lump it?' Puck chimed in, spraying hearts from his fingers. 'Or would fair Sylvie jam his crumpet?'

'Huh?' Will grunted.

'I think so,' said Ani, who seemed able to understand Shakespearean. 'You should have seen them at the Easter bake sale. Monty couldn't get enough of her jam.'

'And what of the matron?' Lady M asked quietly. 'She still seeks the foundling?'

'You what?' Will asked.

'Yes,' Ani translated again. 'So Ms Minola wants to find her daughter. Monty is in love with Sylvie – which is weird, I didn't think you bothered falling in love once you got over, like, thirty, but, hey – and somehow we need to untangle Patrick, Antoine, Hemie and Rosie.'

'And then we need to persuade all of them not to sell their flats to Egeus,' Will added.

'I tell you, you cannot persuade anyone to do anything,' Lady Macbeth insisted. 'It's either in them or it isn't. All you can do is bring it out of them. Or kill them.'

'Yeah . . . probably still not going to take Option B,' Will said. 'Any other advice?'

'Leave it with us,' Yorick sighed. 'We'll put our heads together.'

'We're no fools,' Lady Macbeth insisted.

'The fool thinks they are wise,' came a gentle voice from the door. 'But the wise know themselves to be fools.'

Will spun around to see Ben's mother, Olivia, standing at the doorway in her nightgown, smiling at them and the book. If she was surprised to see four miniature Shakespeareans in an enchanted book, she didn't show it.

'Mistress Olivia,' said Lady Macbeth with a deep curtsey. 'Fare thee well?'

'Very, thank you, m'lady,' said Olivia, returning the curtsey.

'You . . . you know these guys?' Ani asked, voicing the question in Will's head.

'Of course!' Olivia laughed. 'We chat with them all the time, don't we, Rex?'

She turned to Will, who looked to Ani for guidance. She nodded as if to say, *Go with it.*

'Sure,' he replied, gently closing the book. 'All the time.'

'I knew you'd come to see me again,' said Olivia

brightly. 'I've missed you. And don't worry, I have it. I've kept it safe.'

She stepped towards Will and put her hands softly on his face.

'Did you find her?' she whispered.

'Find who?' Will asked.

'Don't worry about it,' Ani said quietly. 'Olivia doesn't always make sense. She says things. We don't always understand them. And we don't think she does either.'

'So much pain,' Olivia said, holding his hand. 'It's time, Rex. Finish your story.'

'Um, OK,' said Will.

'You're a good man,' Olivia said with a smile. 'So kind. You've been so good to me, Rex. So very, very good.'

'Come on, Liv,' sighed Ani. 'Let's get you back to your chair.'

Will tried not to pull a face as Ani took Olivia in her arms and led her back towards her room. Everyone here seemed to think Rex was such a great guy. But he'd been a terrible father to Will's mum. And he hadn't even tried to be a grandfather to him. Some kindness that was—

'What are you doing here?' a suspicious voice asked behind him, making Will jump.

'Oh – er – sorry, I came with Ani,' bumbled Will, Ben's disapproving face making him nervous. 'She said it would be OK, that her mum lets her have friends around all the time.'

'She said what?' Ben interrupted, his voice filled with curious concern.

'That her mum lets her—'

'. . . and so I just don't know if I should tell Ben how your mum really feels,' came Ani's voice from outside the room. 'I mean, she begged me not to say anything, but part of me thinks he has a right to know— Oh! Ben! What are you doing here?'

Will felt his eyes roll. Ani had some good qualities. Subtlety was not one of them. And apparently, acting wasn't another.

'I live here,' Ben said plainly. 'And what are you not telling me, Trouble?'

'Oh, it's nothing,' said Ani airily, twiddling a strand of her hair. 'Just forget about it.'

'Because if that . . . *woman* is up to something,' Ben said darkly, 'then I want to know.'

'She's not up to anything,' Ani said innocently. 'I mean, she's in no fit state, really.'

Will cast his mind back to the Shakespearean characters' suggestion. So Ani was trying to make Ben like his mum. By tricking him. Great plan, like he was going to fall for . . .

'What do you mean?' he asked cautiously. 'No fit state for what?'

Ani tried to look as though she was struggling with what to say.

'OK,' she eventually said. 'But you've got to promise not to say anything. I swore I wouldn't tell you.'

'Wouldn't tell me what?' Ben demanded.

'That she's absolutely crazy about you,' Ani said with a heavy sigh. 'Isn't that right, Will?'

Ani and Ben both looked to Will for confirmation. Will had no idea what to say. So he went with the truth.

'Oh, yeah,' he said eventually. 'You drive her crazy all right.'

'I mean, I just feel so sorry for her,' said Ani, still managing to shoot Will a dirty look. 'She can't eat, she can't sleep, she has no idea what to say to you . . .'

'Well, she didn't have any bother moving several decades of magazines into my parking space!' said Ben indignantly. 'What was the point of that?'

'To get your attention,' Ani shrugged. 'And look how well it's worked! Come on, Ben. It's the oldest trick in the book. You always tease someone you fancy. It's how you find out if they like you back.'

Ben considered this for a moment. Ani smiled. His thoughts were so clear he could have been saying them out loud. Will watched incredulously as this grown, intelligent adult appeared to swallow the absolute tripe that was coming out of this thirteen-year-old girl's mouth. Surely he wasn't going to . . .

Ben snorted a soft laugh.

'Well, that makes a bit more sense of it all,' he smiled. 'I mean, no one can be that petty . . .'

Will thought about the time his mum had ironed parmesan into Uncle Claude's pants after he gave her a five-pound voucher from the supermarket for her birthday. But now wasn't the time.

'But, please, just forget I said anything,' Ani falsely begged. 'She'd rather die than think you know about this.'

Will shook his head. Ani was laying it on with a spade. She'd gone too far.

'I hear you,' Ben said gently. 'And you were right to tell me. I'll tread more softly from here on in. You'd better be getting home, Will. And tell your mum . . . tell her I said hi. If there's anything she wants . . .'

'That's very kind of you,' said Will tactfully, thinking of exactly what his mum would want Ben to do.

'Beach tomorrow?' Ani said brightly as she walked him to the door. 'It's supposed to be another scorcher and the sea is such a nice temperature now.'

Will inwardly groaned as he thought of another day imprisoned in his overheating jumper.

'Sure,' he said. 'See you in the morning.'

'See ya,' said Ani. 'And good work today. I've got a

feeling that everything's going to work out OK.'

Will tried to smile as he walked back to his own flat. He had a lot of feelings about what they'd done that day. And he wasn't convinced any of them were OK.

CHAPTER X

Something Rotten

'We have glad tidings, Master Bard!' Juliet greeted him as he opened his eyes the next morning. 'Verily, we have solved all your woes!'

'Verily you've whatty what now?' Will said groggily. He'd left the *Complete Works* open overnight – the more he got to know them, the harder it was to close the covers on his new friends when he didn't have to. This morning the characters were in Tudor London, the Tower rising majestically from the page, a river of words flowing alongside it.

''Tis true', we have the perfect plan!' Puck enthusiastically agreed. 'Now let's have pizza – mine's deep-pan!'

Puck launched from the page in a shower of paper fireworks and pizza slices.

'It could work,' Yorick moaned. 'Unless you die trying.'

''Tis a masterful plot indeed,' Lady Macbeth confirmed.

'No murders?' Will checked.

'None at all,' Lady Macbeth sighed. 'I said it was masterful. Not perfect.'

'What have you done?' Will asked suspiciously.

'Nothing yet, the day is still young,' Juliet beamed.

'But we swore to help you,' Lady M added. 'And by the day's end, everything shall be fixed.'

'You practising that play again?' his mum's voice asked through the door. 'You're getting really good at that bossy woman's voice.'

Lady Macbeth reached for her dagger. Will shook his head.

'Fine,' she huffed. 'The crone lives.'

'I need you to come and help me sort some papers,' Mary said wearily.

'I'm supposed to be meeting Ani on the beach,' Will objected.

'And I'm supposed to be living on a tropical island with Ryan Gosling,' Mary replied. 'But we don't always get what we want. Boxes. Now.'

'Fine,' sighed Will reluctantly. The faster he did what his mum wanted, the faster he got to do what he wanted. Bitter experience – and a lasting memory of her leaving items of recycling in his bed for a week after he forgot to take the bins out – had taught him that much. 'Coming.'

'I've got to go,' he said to the Shakespeareans. 'You mustn't do *anything* until we've spoken again, you understand?'

The Shakespeareans looked sheepishly amongst themselves.

'I'm serious,' he said seriously. 'Swear it.'

Even as the words came out of his mouth, Will wasn't sure what he was so concerned about. The four of them were stuck to a book, what could they really do?

'So be it,' said Lady Macbeth solemnly. 'We swear that we will do nothing. You have our word.'

The others nodded gravely, Yorick clanking his jawbone as best he could.

'OK,' said Will cautiously. 'I'm going to have to—'

'WILL!' Mary shouted. 'If I have to call you again, I'm putting you in the recycling! Hurry up!'

'Geez, I'm coming,' Will yelled back. 'Give me a second.'

He struggled into his jumper and raced out the room, only remembering at the last second to close his door.

Although, as he would later come to regret, the Bard *didn't* remember to close his book.

Four hours later they were no further forward.

'Wow,' sighed Mary as they waded their way through *1977–1979*. 'In case you were wondering, my parents bought a deep fat fryer in August 1978. Did my father throw anything away?'

'Daughters?' Will grumbled, then wished he hadn't. 'Sorry, I'm just hungry.'

'It's OK,' said Mary. 'I haven't been able to get to the shops today, this job is like a black hole, it sucks you in.'

Will looked resignedly around the room, which seemed to become more littered with paper every hour. They were only supposed to be at Arden Heights for a couple more days, there was no way they were going to get through it all. He pulled out a faded card, with flowers spelling out *Thank You* across the front. Will opened it and read the looping script inside:

For my beloved friends, Violet and Rex.

Thank you, more than I can ever express, for everything you have done for me.

I will never be able to repay your generosity, only your friendship.

Your loving friend (and now neighbour!),

Olivia Touchstone

xxx

‘Olivia Touchstone?’ Will said. ‘That’s Ben’s mum.’

‘What?’ Mary exclaimed, snatching the card from him. ‘No way is that . . . *idiot* Olivia’s son. I refuse to believe it.’

She read the card and smiled.

‘Olivia,’ she said slowly. ‘I’d assumed she’d moved away long ago. She’s still here? In the Heights?’

‘Flat 23,’ Will said cautiously. ‘But I don’t think she’s very well.’

‘Of course, Ben said,’ Mary added quietly. ‘She was so good to me when we used to come here – she’d look after me if my parents were busy. But she didn’t have a son.’

Will recalled the conversation with Ani the day before.

‘Olivia adopted him,’ he explained. ‘She was your babysitter?’ It was always difficult to think of old people being younger. It was like they arrived in the world as adults.

‘Sort of,’ Mary replied. ‘Although she refused to let my parents pay her for it. Said she owed them five years’ rent.’

‘What?’ Will asked. ‘Olivia lived . . . with Rex and Granny?’

‘For a while,’ Mary confirmed. ‘You see, Olivia was forced to leave the country where she was born.’

‘Why?’ asked Will.

Mary shook her head.

'Because some people will always think they have a right to decide where's home and who lives in it,' she said, rootling around the *1972* box. 'Olivia and her brother were forced to flee for their lives. Sadly, only Olivia made it to our shores.'

Mary pulled out a local newspaper clipping, appealing for people to host displaced families who were living in the church.

'Mum and Dad saw this and went straight to St Crispin's,' Mary continued. 'They saw Olivia there all alone and their hearts went out to her. I think my father related to her – he too had lost a brother. Did I ever tell you that?'

'No?' said Will. This was the longest conversation they'd ever had about Rex. There was a lot he didn't know.

'It was tragic,' Mary sighed. 'You see, your grandfather grew up in terrible poverty – his father died in the war and his mother struggled to bring two boys up alone. Rex's brother, Edmund, got ill. In those days, medicine was very expensive and his mother hoped it was just a cold. But it wasn't. And one day, Edmund didn't wake up.'

'Oh,' said Will, not sure what else he could say. For the first time in his life, he felt a pang of sympathy for Rex. Although not far behind it came another, less generous thought.

If Rex knew what it was like to lose family, why did he choose to abandon his daughter?

'This became your grandfather's motivation,' she said. 'He studied and studied, got himself into grammar school and then university – you could do that for free in those days – and his college employed him. And there he met a sparky young scientist who was showing the boys who was boss . . .'

'Granny,' Will grinned.

'The very same,' Mary smiled. 'She blazed a trail for female scientists – and my father was right behind her. They both believed passionately in the power of education, as did Olivia. So they brought her here and she stayed with them until she was able to get on her feet. Which she did – she was a maths whizz – not that people would acknowledge her qualifications when she first arrived. So she did them all again, graduated with a first and eventually became a financial director for a big clothes chain. Here.'

She pulled a photo out of *1976*. The faces were new, but not unfamiliar. They were younger versions of Rex, Violet and Olivia. And they looked really happy.

'I'm guessing this was all your mum's idea,' said Will, handing the clipping back. 'Doesn't sound like something Rex would do.'

'You might be surprised what Rex did,' said Mary. 'Your grandfather was a huge champion of the underdog. He knew what it was like when life hadn't been fair and he was determined to make it fairer for others.'

'Unless they were his own child,' Will said, not sorry this time.

Mary sighed deeply.

'So it would seem,' she said, just as the doorbell went. 'I'll go – I'm getting a numb bum sitting here.'

Mary rose stiffly from the floor with a groan, and opened the front door.

'Good morning,' came the slow, solemn voice from a man dressed entirely in black. 'Father Laurence Lodowick. I'm here to see Monty. Sorry I'm a bit late, never can seem to keep track of time.'

'Oh, I'm afraid you have the wrong flat,' Mary replied to the priest. 'And I don't know where—'

'He's in flat 11,' Will chipped in. 'Is . . . is everything OK?'

'Absolutely. I have everything in hand,' the priest promised. 'Flat 7, you said?'

'Eleven,' Mary repeated. 'Would you like me to show you the way?'

'No need,' said the priest amiably. 'I always get where I need to be. Eventually. Flat 21, here I come!'

'Eleven!' Mary shouted down the corridor after him.

'I said *eleven.* Oh, well. I'm sure he'll find his way. Go on, kiddo, you should get out of here too. You've put in a shift, weren't you supposed to meet Ani?'

Will saw the time.

'Oh, no – I'm late,' he said. 'And I'm sure she'll have nothing to say about that.'

'Nothing at all,' Mary added with a wink. 'Always hard to know what that one's thinking.'

His fingers sore from paper cuts, Will was happy to be released into the warm afternoon. He was about to head through the gardens when he was stopped by a lost delivery man.

'Excuse me, mate,' he called to Will. 'Ariel Deliveries. Looking for Arden Heights.'

'You found it,' Will said.

'Oh, thank goodness for that,' he said, going to the back of his van and pulling out two boxes. 'These cakes won't survive long in this heat. And you can't have a tea dance without cake.'

Will smiled to himself as he thought of the drama that cake was already causing at the Heights.

'If you go down to the lawns, I think they're setting up the tea dance there,' Will instructed. 'But make sure you don't run.'

'Thanks, pal,' said the man cheerfully. 'Appreciate your time.'

'No worries,' said Will, continuing on his way. He was just heading through the garden towards the steps to the beach, when he heard two women talking loudly on a bench.

It was Sylvie from flat 34. And she was with Angela.

'I don't know what else to tell you, dearie,' Angela said sincerely, although something about it wasn't at all sincere. 'Monty doesn't feel that way about you.'

Will hesitated and walked more slowly to listen to the conversation. And he didn't like what he was hearing. And nor, it appeared, did Sylvie.

'Yer what?' said Sylvie.

'I SAID,' Angela shouted. 'MONTY DOESN'T FEEL THAT WAY ABOUT YOU.'

Sylvie recoiled at both the volume and the content.

'Oh, I'm such a silly old fool,' Sylvie said, a few tears starting to come. 'I was so sure he liked me.'

'Well, I hate to be the one to break it you,' Angela replied, handing her a handkerchief and looking incredibly pleased with herself. 'But it's clearly time to move on. You'd best forget him.'

'Yer what?' Sylvie asked. 'I need to baguette him?'

'YOU NEED TO FORGET HIM!' Angela spelt out.

'Ah, I dunno,' Sylvie sniffed. 'Monty's just . . . so

lovely. A real ray of sunshine, innit? And so charming.'

'Oh, he's charming all right,' said Angela archly. 'Why, at the Pot Luck Supper, I saw him cosying up to Hemie from flat 10. 'Offered to get her some ham and leek pie.'

'Yer what?' Sylvie asked. 'He offered some pee in her eye?!'

'HAM AND LEEK PIE!' Angela shouted impatiently.

Sylvie shook her head.

'I just can't believe it,' she said. 'Things were going so well. I was going to ask him out. They do a lovely early-bird supper down the Globe – pensioners get soup of the day and a free hot fudge sundae. And you can still get home in time for *Coronation Street*. Maybe I should ask him, just to be sure.'

'Well, you can, dearie,' said Angela, straightening her skirt. 'But I'd be no sort of friend if I sat back and let you. Especially when I heard . . . No, it's none of my business, Sylvie. It's your life.'

'Yer what?' said Sylvie. 'He's not my wife.'

'IT'S YOUR LIFE,' Angela shouted. 'BUT JUST THE OTHER DAY I OVERHEARD HIM COMPLIMENTING MEG FROM FLAT 22! ON HER RASPBERRY JAM!'

'No!' Sylvie gasped.

'I'M AFRAID SO,' Angela yelled. 'HE SAID . . . HE SAID IT WAS THE BEST HE'D EVER TASTED!'

'He DID NOT!' Sylvie outraged. 'The lying, two-faced

. . . He said that MY raspberry jam was the best he'd ever tasted!'

'Oh, maybe I made a mistake,' said Angela, although Will caught the smile on her lips.

'Yer what?' Sylvie asked. 'He's weighed a steak?'

'NO,' Angela yelled with a sigh. 'I JUST THINK YOU SHOULD–'

'Don't you worry, Ange,' Sylvie huffed. 'I've heard you loud and clear.'

'Thank goodness for that,' Angela said under her breath. 'Anyway, I'd better go. I've been invited to a leadership seminar this afternoon, "Know Your Fate". It's run by three sisters, all about female empowerment.'

'I need to get off an' all,' said Sylvie, standing up. 'Well, I hope Monty enjoys Meg and her acidic jam. I'm telling you, she uses far too much lemon juice. Peri from flat 33 keeps asking me round for tea. So I'm going to make him my very best spiced plum! And I bet he won't say no to a hot fudge sundae!'

Sylvie stormed off, Angela grinning to herself as she followed in her wake.

Will hesitated, his ears ringing with what he'd just heard. Should he speak up? Stop Sylvie and tell her the truth? Would she even believe a total stranger?

But instead, he walked on towards the beach steps. He didn't have the words and he wouldn't know what to do with them if he did.

Because if there was one thing Will Davenant knew, it was how to keep quiet.

'Seriously? What a snake!' Ani cried as Will relayed the conversation he'd just witnessed when he reached the beach. 'I'm going to go straight up there and—'

'No, you're not,' Will said, holding her back. 'Let's stop and think before blundering in.'

'The fact is,' Ani said defiantly, 'Angela is lying! You heard Monty, he's crazy about Sylvie! People who love each other should be together! This isn't right!'

'It isn't,' Will said. 'But if you go in all guns blazing, you might make it worse. Let's just wait. We will help Monty. But let's make sure we're actually helping.'

Ani sat with a face like a chewed wasp.

'All right,' she scowled. 'Let's at least have a swim, though. I am Not Happy.'

'I'd never have guessed,' said Will. 'But it's too late to swim now, it'll be dinner soon and—'

'We've got loads of time,' Ani declared. 'The water's still lovely. Come on in, you must be boiling.'

'Forgot my swim shorts!' Will said, slapping his forehead. 'Urgh. Must have left my brain in one of Rex's boxes.'

‘Seriously?’ said Ani. Will wasn’t sure if there was suspicion in her voice. But he didn’t really want to look for it. And he certainly didn’t want to find it.

‘I’m fine,’ he said, trying to ignore the inviting cool sea before him. ‘I don’t really like swimming anyway.’

A vision of him and his dad mucking around in the water flitted into his mind. He quickly threw it out the other side.

‘OK,’ said Ani, definitely suspicious this time. ‘Well, Ben gave me some money for ice creams – he’s in a really good mood today. I think it’s because of your mum.’

‘Yeah, about that,’ Will began. ‘I’m not sure this is such a good idea. It’s only a matter of time until he discovers that you – and me, because you’ve now dragged me into it – made it all up. And they’re both going to kill us when they do. With or without Lady M’s help.’

‘You need to lighten up,’ Ani chided. ‘Everything will be fine. Especially with a double whippy with two flakes and sprinkles. Like I say, Ben’s in a *really* good mood today.’

Will waited while Ani gathered up her belongings, before joining her on the short walk to the bright blue ice cream stand a little further along the front.

‘So what’s the deal with Ben?’ Will asked.

‘Whaddya mean?’ Ani asked.

‘How come you’re staying with him?’

'Like I said, family friend,' Ani said quickly.

'But you said you'd been here for months – you met Rex,' Will probed. 'That's a long time to stay with a friend.'

'Look,' said Ani, stopping and turning to him. 'It's not that deep. My mum goes away with work a lot. I can't always go with her. Ben's a mate and he looks after me. End. Of. Story.'

'OK,' said Will. 'Sorry. I didn't mean to pry.'

'So don't,' said Ani angrily, continuing the walk in silence.

Will looked out over the sea. Thanks to his mum's captive working programme, he'd missed most of the day, but this did also mean that most of the tourists had left. By the time they got to the ice-cream stand, only one person stood in front of them.

'Result,' Ani said brightly, her anger apparently passed over like a cloud across the sun. 'The queue for this place is usually halfway across the sea. Now do I want blue sauce or pink? Hmmmm.'

Will was surveying the delicious array of options before him when his attention was drawn away by the man in front of them. It was Caleb. And he was smiling.

'Lovely day,' he said, tucking into the three scoops of chocolate ice cream in his cup as he walked away. 'Enjoy your ice creams.'

Will looked at Ani, who was just as confused as he was.

'Er, thanks,' said Ani in bewilderment. 'See you around, Caleb.'

Caleb stopped dead in his tracks, as frozen as the ice cream in his hands.

'Caleb?' he said, slowly turning around. 'You know him?'

Will wondered how to handle this. He knew that senior citizens could get a little confused from time to time – look at Olivia. But this man didn't look confused. He looked . . . intrigued. It was super-weird. As ever, Ani found the words he couldn't.

'Um . . . you don't?' she said, which Will had to admit was as good a way to handle it as any.

The man smiled sadly.

'I used to,' he said, his head dropping. 'You see, Caleb is my brother.'

CHAPTER XI

The Tragedy of Errors

Will took in the man before him. He was identical in every way to the Arden Heights caretaker in appearance. But his demeanour couldn't have been more different.

'You're . . . you're twins?' Ani clarified.

'We are,' he confirmed with a sad smile. 'Twenty-two minutes apart in birth. Forty-five years apart in life. My name is Anthony. Nice to meet you both.'

They all looked awkwardly amongst one another for a moment. Will wasn't sure how to handle this delicate situation. He remembered the story that Caleb's brother had stolen his family business from him. You never could tell what people were truly like. But this guy didn't seem like a bully or a thief. He seemed like a decent man. Who really liked chocolate ice cream. Will didn't know what to say.

But, of course, he didn't have to.

'So what happened?' Ani waded in.

Anthony smiled kindly.

'Why don't I get you both an ice cream and we can talk about it?'

Will was about to enthusiastically accept, when Ani stepped in again.

'We can't take an ice cream from a stranger, thank you,' she said. 'But if you want to go and sit on that bench where everyone can see us, we'd love to hear your story.'

Anthony nodded.

'You are a very wise young woman,' he said seriously. 'See you in a moment.'

Will and Ani garbled their order at the ice-cream vendor – double flake with blue sauce for Ani, two scoops of vanilla with pink sauce for Will – and headed over to talk to Anthony.

'I must ask, how on earth do you know my brother?' he began, once they'd settled themselves down.

'He lives in our block of flats,' said Ani. 'It's . . . Ar—'

'It's a really good place to live,' Will interrupted. This man seemed nice. But Ani was right to be cautious, they shouldn't be giving their – or Caleb's – address out to complete strangers. Ani held the words in her mouth. She seemed to understand the point. That made a change.

'So he came back too,' sighed Anthony, more to himself than his audience. 'Interesting.'

Will waited for Anthony to continue. Ani didn't.

'Why?' she asked.

'Our parents used to bring us here as children,' he said. 'We lived in a big city, hours from here. And my family had very little. But every summer, without fail, we'd come here for the weekend – that was our summer holiday. A tradition I have kept with my own family.'

'So . . . you've been in the same place for years and you've never run into each other?' Ani asked. 'That's weird.'

'Not really,' Anthony sighed. 'Life can be very good at hiding people. Especially if they don't want to be found.'

Will thought about Rex and his mum. They managed to hide from each other for years. Even though they knew exactly where the other was.

'What happened between you?' Ani asked. 'I heard you took the family business from him – no offence.'

'What?' said Anthony incredulously. 'Caleb told you that?'

'No,' said Will, sensing Anthony's hurt and not wanting to add to it. 'It was just what we heard. Second hand. Maybe second-hundred hand, who knows?'

'Ah, yes,' said Anthony. 'Stories don't always travel well and rarely arrive in one piece. And both sides are unlikely to survive the journey.'

He took a spoonful of his ice cream and looked out over the sea. His resemblance to his twin was extraordinary, Will wouldn't have been able to tell them apart. At least until he ran down a hallway.

'As with all tales, there is a seed of truth in there,' Anthony began. 'I did inherit the family business from my father. Caleb had never taken any great interest in making gloves – that's our family trade. My brother was more interested in poetry.'

'POETRY?' Ani exclaimed, spitting out a mouthful of ice cream. 'Caleb?!'

'Oh, yes,' Anthony smiled. 'He had quite the talent. Wrote over one hundred and fifty poems, last I knew.'

'Wow,' Ani said, shaking her head. 'I thought the only words Caleb knew were "clear" and "off".'

'He always did have a more . . . challenging side,' Anthony chuckled. 'But then, all great artists tend to.'

Anthony took another bite of his ice cream, reminding Will to try his before it melted in the hazy evening heat. It had been so long since he'd tasted ice cream, Will had totally forgotten that perfect blend of sweet creaminess that melted on his tongue and delighted his soul. It was such a simple pleasure. But it had been a while since he'd enjoyed many pleasures, simple or otherwise.

'Anyway, when our father passed, he left the business

to me,' Anthony continued. 'He and Caleb had always had a difficult relationship and Caleb had left home under a cloud some years earlier. I was working with my father at the factory, had married and had young children – I think my father thought he was doing the right thing. Or didn't think at all.'

'I can kinda see Caleb's point, though,' said Ani, apparently feeling qualified to have an opinion about something she'd known for two whole minutes. 'I mean, even if he and your dad didn't get on, he was still entitled to his share, no?'

Will thought about this. His mum was surely entitled to something from her father. She had just accepted that everything was going to Claude. That didn't seem fair. If anything, she was owed more. Why didn't she fight?

'I quite agree,' said Anthony. 'And I wrote to Caleb and told him so. Many times, in fact. I invited him to come and work with me, or at least to take what was rightfully his. But he never replied to my letters. Like I say, he was often challenging. And stubborn as a mule – although we're both guilty of that.'

'Didn't you try to find him?' Will asked. 'Try to sort it out?'

Anthony dropped his head.

'I'm ashamed to say that I didn't. Not nearly as hard as I might have done,' he admitted. 'I was a younger, more foolish man. I felt I'd tried and if my brother was going to be pig-headed, then so was I. I always meant to resolve it one day. But that's the problem with One Day. Before you know it, it becomes Never. And for forty-five years, there's been a question mark. Where there should have been a brother.'

Anthony went to have another bite of ice cream. But he seemed to have lost his appetite.

'Look,' said Ani. 'Perhaps we could help? We know Caleb – we could try to talk to him? If you wanted us to?'

Anthony's eyes clouded over.

'What's the point?' he said. 'If my brother had wanted to find me these past decades, I'm sure he could have found a way. He obviously doesn't want anything to do with me.'

'Isn't it better to know for sure?' Ani pushed. 'I mean, it's hard. But at least then you'd have a full stop rather than a question mark?'

Their new acquaintance laughed.

'Out of the mouths of babes,' he said gently.

'Eh?' Ani replied.

'Why don't you give us your contact details?' Will suggested, again cautious about giving too much away to someone who was still a stranger. 'That way, Caleb can get in touch with you if he wants to.'

Anthony smiled at them both.

'You are very kind young people,' he said, pulling his wallet and taking a business card out of it. 'And whatever happens, I'm grateful for that.'

Ani took the card from his hand and read it.

'Wow!' she said. 'You make gloves for the Royal Family?! You must be loaded!'

Anthony laughed again. Will groaned.

'Do you have any filter between your brain and your mouth?' he asked.

'I like it,' said Anthony, finishing his ice cream and standing to leave. 'It's refreshing to have someone speak their mind.'

'Careful what you wish for,' Will muttered, earning him a shove from Ani.

'I must get back to my family,' Anthony said. 'But I'm glad to have met you, my young friends. I wish you every happiness. Thank you for your time.'

Will watched as Anthony deposited his ice-cream pot in the bin, then made his way slowly along the front.

'How weird is that?' Ani said, as they walked back to Arden Heights. 'That two twins should end up in the same small place? I wonder what Caleb's going to make of it when you talk to him.'

'I dunno,' sighed Will. 'It'll be really . . . Hold on, why am *I* talking to him?'

Ani shrugged.

'I think he'll respond better to you than me,' she said. 'He hates me.'

'Caleb hates everyone,' Will pointed out.

'True,' Ani agreed. 'But he's really had it in for me since I a little bit skateboarded around the car park and scuffed up his new tarmac. You're fresh meat. He hasn't had time to hate you as much. Yet.'

'Gee, thanks,' said Will, taking Anthony's card and putting it in his jeans pocket. He hoped it would survive in there. Even his sweat was sweating in this heat.

The rest of the journey back to Arden Heights was spent discussing the vote and how they could persuade Ms Minola and Monty to vote against the development. It was certainly more constructive than Will's conversation with the Shakespeareans. With considerably less murder involved, which was a bonus.

But no sooner had they rounded the corner to the Arden Heights gardens, than they were nearly mown down by Antoine and Rosie.

'What are they doing?' Will asked as strains of violin music wafted across the lawn.

'I think it's the tango,' Ani replied as the dance partners spun around and started charging back the other way. 'Look out!'

'Oh, Antoine!' Rosie exclaimed joyfully, as Will and Ani leapt out of their path. 'It's like dancing with an angel! You're a geriatric John Travolta!'

She ripped a rose from a nearby bush, put it between her teeth and dipped Antoine violently backwards.

'Ooooh! Thank you, love,' groaned Antoine, 'but watch me dicky hip.'

'That's weird,' Ani said. 'I thought Rosie was super into Patrick. Just like Hemie.'

'Maybe not,' said Will, gesturing across the lawn. 'Look sharp.'

Across the lawn, Hemie was dancing – dragging, really – Patrick towards them. It was less of a tango. More a tactical assault.

'Well, this makes a change from the Viennese waltz,' Patrick panted. 'Although look at the weeds in those begonias.'

Giving Hemie a spin, Patrick wandered off towards his precious flowers, meaning that Hemie kept on spinning . . . until she spun straight into Antoine.

'Ooof, mind how you go, love,' said Antoine, catching her before she could fall.

Will grimaced as Hemie's face melted like warm jelly.

'Oh, Antoine!' Hemie gasped. 'You're so . . . manly.'

'Give over!' said Antoine.

'Uh-oh,' said Ani quietly. 'It's all going to kick off again.'

'You are, Anty,' said Rosie, pushing Hemie away. 'And

you're all mine. So Hemie? Back off, baggy bum!'

'How dare you!' Hemie roared. 'Don't you stand between me and my true love!'

'Yer what?' Antoine said, confused.

'I love you, Antoine!' Hemie declared. 'From the core of my being! From the depths of my soul to the top of my stairlift! I am yours!'

'Keep your wrinkly hands to yourself,' said Rosie, pulling a terrified Antoine to her. 'He's mine!'

'He. Is. Not!' Hemie cried, yanking Antoine back to her. 'He's mine!'

'Anyone fancy a foxtrot?' said Patrick, strolling over amiably.

'No!' said both the women together, pulling Antoine between them like a Christmas cracker.

'What is going on?' Will asked, just as a shout rose up from a balcony above.

'SYLVIE!' a booming Italian voice came rolling across the gardens. 'EIGHTY-FOUR ART THOU SYLVIE . . . Eh? What's this now? Oh, sorry, my mistake . . . WHEREFORE ART THOU, SYLVIE?'

Will looked at Ani, who returned his bemused stare.

'Monty?' they said at once and ran around the building. There, arms outstretched on his own balcony, was their Italian friend. And just behind him, was Father Laurence.

'SYLVIE!' Monty yelled again. 'SPEAK TO ME, MY LOVE!'

A set of French doors opened two floors above and Sylvie came shuffling out.

'Monty!' she called up. 'Is that you?'

'IT IS!' Monty replied, as the priest whispered in his ear. 'DENY YOUR FATHER AND REFUSE YOUR NAME!'

'YOU WHAT?' Sylvie shouted back.

'I SAY,' Monty shouted back, 'DENY YOUR FATHER AND REFUSE YOUR NAME!'

'REFRY MY LARDER AND DEFUSE MY FLAME?!' Sylvie yelled back. 'WHAT YOU ON ABOUT, YOU DAFT BEGGAR?!'

'SYLVIE! *BELLA* SYLVIE!' Monty cried. 'I HAVE TO TELL YOU, I LOVE YOU!'

Sylvie looked confused.

'YOU ARE NOT ABOVE ME!' she shouted back. 'I'D WANTED ONE OF THE FLATS ON THE GROUND FLOOR, WHAT WITH MY DODGY KNEE AND ALL!'

'OH, NO! IS YOUR ARTHRITIS FLARING UP AGAIN?' Monty yelled back. 'PERHAPS YOU NEED SOME COLD PEAS?'

'IT'S NONE OF YOUR BUSINESS IF I NEED A PEE!' Sylvie yelled back. 'AND BESIDES, I'M NOT SPEAKING TO YOU, YOU JAM TART!'

Monty looked lost.

'WHATEVER DO YOU MEAN?' he called. 'I ONLY HAVE EYES FOR YOU!'

'YOU WHAT?'

'I SAY . . . MONTY ONLY HAS EYES FOR YOU!'

'DON'T YOU TALK TO ME ABOUT PIES!' Sylvie shouted back. 'I KNOW MONTY'S GOT PIES FOR EVERYONE!'

'BUT, SYLVIE!' Monty cried desperately.

'ENOUGH!' Sylvie shouted back. 'I'VE GOT FISH GOUJONS IN THE OVEN AND IT'S *ANTIQUES ROAD-SHOW* IN FIVE MINUTES!'

'BUT, SYLVIE!' Monty cried after her. 'SYLVIE! MY LOVE!'

'I HAVEN'T SEEN YER GLOVE!' Sylvie yelled back. 'AND I DON'T WANT TO SEE YOU NEITHER! NOW SHOVE OFF!'

And with that, Sylvie shuffled back inside her flat and shut the door.

'Oh, no,' said Ani. 'Poor guy. Told you we should have talked to Sylvie. Now Monty's heart is broken and it's all your fault.'

Ani might have been right. Or she might have been wrong. But Will had a bigger concern.

'Come on, we need to get back to mine,' he said. 'I've got a bad feeling I know who has the full story here.'

'The Shakespeareans?' Ani asked, running alongside him. 'But how?'

'Who knows?' Will replied. 'But we need to find out.'

They ran into the Heights and up the stairs towards the second floor, nearly knocking Julian flying as they hurtled past on the stairs.

'Sorry!' Ani called back. 'You OK?!'

'Absolutely super!' Julian beamed. 'Just on my way to chair my first residents' committee meeting. Wish me luck!'

'Good luck!' they shouted in unison as they reached their floor. They had just slammed the door to flat 29 behind them and were about to go into Will's room when there was a frantic knocking at the front door.

'What now?' Ani said, striding back towards the front door, apparently unperturbed by the fact that this wasn't actually her home.

'Wait – we don't know who—' Will began, remembering that it's generally a bad idea to open a door to someone who is trying to hammer it down.

But even he was surprised who they found on the other side.

'Ms Minola?' Ani said, looking at the woman, who was thrusting her phone towards them. 'Are you OK?'

'I've got a virus!' she screamed in delight.

'Er, congratulations,' Will said, slightly confused as

Ani took the phone.

'Oh my goodness!' said Ani, her eyes growing wider than Ms Minola's screen. 'You mean you've gone viral! That post about Bianca! It's been reposted thousands of times, tens of thousands of times! This is incredible!'

'I know!' shrieked Ms Minola, whose usually frowning face was lit up with a crazed joy. 'You did it!'

'Did what?' Will asked, joining Ani in peering at the screen.

'You found her!' Ms Minola shouted in their faces. 'She's just messaged me! Children! You found my Bianca!'

CHAPTER XII

Love is Blind

With Mary out at the shops, Will and Ani led Ms Minola through to flat 29's front room. Ms M, who usually used her words rather sparingly, didn't stop babbling the entire time Will was clearing some space for them to sit down – talking about what should she wear and where should they go and something about scones that Will didn't entirely understand. She was frantic.

'OK, so,' said Ani, taking the phone from Ms Minola's trembling hands once Will had decluttered *1995–1997*. 'Let's do a few checks here. Who is saying she's your daughter?'

'She's not *saying* she's Bianca. She is!' Ms Minola said. 'Look, she's right there!'

'Bianca . . . Minola,' Will said suspiciously. 'Her name

was never changed?'

'No!' Ms Minola practically shrieked. 'She still there! She's still my Bianca! Look, there's a picture and everything! She's got my eyes!'

Will looked at Bianca's profile. It was true, she bore a striking resemblance to her mother. Too much of one, perhaps . . .

Ani was scrolling on the phone. And looked like she had her doubts too.

'Ms Minola, this is a bit weird,' she said, a little guiltily, Will thought. 'This profile, it only started today. There's no history, no way of finding out anything about her.'

'Well, someone must have told her about me and she made one up!' Ms Minola cried. 'And just look at the picture! You can see the apple hasn't fallen very far from the tree!'

'People can make pictures up, Ms Minola,' Will said quietly. 'Someone could have taken that old picture of you and used artificial intelligence to create what your daughter might have looked like. And if she hasn't changed her name, why couldn't you find her all these years?'

'No!' said Ms Minola firmly, her more familiar angry face clouding over her wild smile. 'This is my Bianca! I can feel it! She's coming tomorrow – and on her birthday! She's found me! We've found each other!'

'And that's wonderful if you have,' Ani said softly. 'But all we're saying is that you should just be a bit careful, there are a lot of bad—'

'But . . . but . . . this was all your idea,' said the older woman in confusion. 'Yesterday you were all for it.'

'I'm all for you finding your Bianca,' Ani clarified. 'I still am. And I really want her to find you too. Everyone deserves a mum. But the internet can be a strange place, Will's right, I hadn't really thought it all through. I can be a bit like that.'

'I knew you wouldn't understand!' said Ms Minola, gathering up her phone and pulling herself off the sofa. 'But now I've got my Bianca back and that's all that matters!'

'Ms Minola, wait,' Ani urged, rushing after her irate neighbour. 'Please, we're only trying to help.'

The formidable woman turned and looked hatefully at the young girl before her.

'I don't need your help,' she hissed. 'I never did. Now leave me alone.'

Ms Minola stormed towards the front door. Ani made to go after her again, but Will put a hand on her arm.

'Leave her,' he said. 'She's angry. She won't listen now.'

'But . . . what if this "Bianca" isn't who she says she is?' Ani said, panic-stricken. 'What if I've put Ms Minola in danger? What if she gets in trouble? What if—'

'Everything OK in here?' Mary asked, walking through the door with a bag of groceries. 'Ani – you all right?'

'I'm fine,' Ani replied, plastering a smile on her face.

'You sure?' Mary asked with concern.

'Sure,' said Ani. 'Everything's fine.'

'If you say so,' said Mary, waving the grocery bag. 'Would you like to stay for dinner? It's nothing fancy, I'm afraid. But Will can tell you I make a mean cheesy pasta.'

'Thanks, I'd—'

Ani stopped. Will watched a face that had moments ago been darkened by worry, light right back up again. It was extraordinary how quickly her moods could come and go, like storms that blow themselves out over the sea. And Will recognized this new mood. Ani was up to something.

'I'd have loved to, Mary,' she said, in a weird, flat tone. 'But I'm going to have to go. Ben needs some help. He wants to get exactly the right present for— Oh, no! Me and my big mouth!'

Ani clamped her hands dramatically to her lips. Will was confused. What was she doing?

'I'm so sorry – I was supposed to keep it a secret,' Ani sighed. 'I'm such a big mouth.'

'You got that right,' Will muttered. 'What are you—'

‘Ben asks one thing of me, “don’t tell Mary I’ve got a crush on her”,’ Ani said, Will now recognizing her terrible acting voice. ‘And here I am, blabbing away.’

Will didn’t need to look at his mum. He knew Mary wasn’t stupid enough to–

‘I’m sorry, what?’ she said with a small smile. ‘Are you trying to tell me that Ben . . . likes me?’

‘Actually, I’m trying not to tell you that,’ Ani said with a fake frown. ‘But I’m not doing a very good job, am I?’

Will rolled his eyes. Ani was so obvious. But he needn’t worry. Ben might have fallen for this rubbish. But there was no way his mum was going to.

‘Really?’ Mary asked curiously. ‘Are you sure? He acts like he hates me.’

‘Men,’ said Ani with a pronounced eye roll. ‘Am I right? I can only apologize. I think Ben’s a bit out of practice. His last girlfriend was in, like, 1564. But this is how I know how much he likes you. The angrier he is, the more he’s into you.’

Will couldn’t help but release an incredulous splutter. This was complete nonsense. He was going to put a stop to it right now.

‘Mum,’ he said, shooting Ani a look that warned her not to say another word. ‘I have to . . .’

But before he could get his words out, he saw Mary’s face. She was smiling. Really, properly, actually smiling.

He hadn't seen that for a while.

'Interesting,' she said. 'That explains a lot.'

It was on the tip of his tongue to tell his mum that she was being played, that Ani was tricking her and this was all complete rubbish.

But then he saw the smile again.

And he couldn't bring himself to do it.

'I'm telling you, there's something in the water in the Heights today,' Mary said as Will took the shopping bag from her. 'Love is in the air.'

'What do you mean?' he asked as he started to unpack the shopping.

'Didn't you hear Monty yelling his love for Sylvie?' Mary giggled. 'And it's all kicking off at the tea dance. There's something up around here.'

Will and Ani exchanged knowing glances. They needed to talk to the Shakespeareans.

'Well, if you can wait for dinner, kiddo, I need a quick bath, I'm gross,' said his mum right on cue. 'Catch you later, Ani.'

Mary headed into the bathroom and shut the door. The moment he and Ani heard the taps running, they ran into the bedroom and grabbed the book, finding the Shakespeareans warming themselves by a paper fire in a grand Scottish castle.

'What have you done?' Will demanded, making them

all jump out of their chairs.

'*We* have done nothing,' Lady Macbeth said archly.

'What does that mean?' Ani asked suspiciously. 'Juliet?'

Will joined Ani in staring intently at the youngest character, also confident that Juliet would break first.

'Well, Master Will,' she said, looking guiltily at the others. 'You had our sworn word that *we* wouldn't do anything. So we might have, a little bit, even verily . . .'

'We got some of the others to do it for us,' Yorick groaned. 'We're no use to anyone here, might as well be dead.'

'You kind of *are* dead,' Ani pointed out.

'Gee, thanks,' Yorick moaned. 'I've still got some feelings, you know.'

'Help how?' Will asked firmly.

'We told you we could send a letter,' said Puck, sending a shower of golden letters off the page. 'We asked our friends to make all better!'

'Our friend Titus runs the most wonderful restaurant – we asked him to whip up a few cakes for the tea dance,' Juliet clapped happily. 'And they are full of wild pansy juice! It's the most potent love potion in the world!'

'You. Did. What?' Will said slowly. 'It's bad enough watching Ani's performance as Worst Matchmaker Ever – but drugging people, that's just wrong.'

'Be not afeard and do not weep,' Puck said. 'The potion shall fade with a little sleep.'

Will considered how many times a day the Arden Heights residents took a nap. This was good news.

'OK,' he said, 'so is that what you've done to Monty too?'

'Oh, no,' Juliet said earnestly. 'I asked my dear old friend, Friar Laurence to pay him a visit. He's always full of the best ideas. When he finally gets to the right place.'

'Clearly,' said Ani. 'Well, look, so a few people tangoed over cupcakes and Monty's going to have a bit of a sore throat tomorrow, it could be worse.'

Will wanted to share her enthusiasm. But one look at the guilty Shakespeareans told him there was still more to this story.

'Go on,' he sighed. 'Out with it.'

They all looked to Lady Macbeth, who stood forward defiantly.

'This Egeus business – the residents' committee needs to grow a backbone,' she declared. 'This nonsense should have been stopped long ago. They need vision. They need action. They need leadership.'

'They've got leadership. Julian was elected the other night,' Ani pointed out.

Lady Macbeth shook her head.

'They need proper leadership. They need someone

who will get the job done. Someone who will not hesitate to make the difficult judgements. Someone strong and brave and decisive.'

She looked squarely at Will.

'They need a woman.'

A snatched moment from earlier swept across Will's mind.

'Angela,' he said. 'That talk she was going to about leadership?'

'Run by three good friends of mine,' Lady Macbeth said unapologetically. 'They do excellent motivational talks – *The Three Whiches?* – inspirational stuff. I thought they could give Angela a few suggestions about taking a firmer hand with the committee. But I've said my piece. I can wash my hands of the whole business.'

'Oh, no,' said Ani. 'You heard Julian – there's a residents' committee meeting going on right now. What do you think Angela will do?'

'I don't know,' said Will, 'but we'd better get down there and find out. You lot. Urgh . . . I'll deal with you later.'

He slammed the book shut and raced after Ani as she pelted out of the door.

'Hey, where do you think you're going?' Mary said, emerging from the bathroom in a towel as they sprinted past. 'What about dinner?'

'I'll be back soon,' Will said quickly, before running out of the door to Ani. 'But I smell trouble. And it's not just Mum's cheesy pasta.'

CHAPTER XIII

Et Tu, Angela?

'No running in the corridors!' Caleb yelled after them as they raced down the hallway towards the stairs. 'Someone's gonna get hurt!'

Will wanted to stop and talk to the caretaker, he had so much to tell him. But first they needed to find out what – if anything – Angela was going to do. They took the stairs to the ground floor and the recreation room where the residents' committee meeting was to be held.

'Should we go in?' Will asked as they hesitated outside.

'And say what?' Ani pointed out. 'No, let's keep an eye for a minute, see how things play out. We could be worrying over nothing.'

Will nodded, but was far from certain. There was something about Angela. The way she'd been at the meeting, the way she'd been with Sylvie – he didn't trust her. Not one bit.

'And so,' said Julian, standing at the head of the oval table, which the other members of the committee were sitting around. 'I am delighted to be chairing my first meeting as head of this wonderful committee! I'm so very grateful for your votes and I will do my very best to be as good and conscientious a leader as Rex was before me. Now, the first order of business is a small technicality. Henry King has divided flat 2 into two parts. The postman is having a terrible time with the mail and the post office are insisting we give the second flat a number. Any suggestions? What about 2A?'

The committee began shouting out their thoughts.

'Yes!'

'No!'

'2B, or . . .'

'Not 2B!'

'That is the question,' Julian pondered.

'Erm, excuse me, Mr Chairman,' Angela piped up in her sugary voice. 'Before we can commit to anything, we have to unanimously confirm the result of yesterday's vote to officially appoint you as chair.'

Julian slapped a hand to his head.

'Thank the heavens for you, Angela. I'd lose my head if it wasn't screwed on,' he said jovially, to a cool nod from Angela.

'Have you got a bad feeling about this?' Ani whispered.

'Massively,' Will confirmed as Julian started to speak again.

'You are, of course, entirely correct,' Julian continued. 'Sorry, chaps, just a bit of admin. If I could have a show of hands to make yesterday's election official.'

All the hands around the table went up. Except for one.

'Angela?' said Julian pleasantly. 'I know it's a bore doing anything in this heat. But for the sake of the records, I will need your—'

'I'm afraid I cannot do that,' Angela said with a terrifying smile.

'Oh, love,' said Coral. 'Is it your tennis elbow? I had a terrible time with mine after that over-seventies salsa.'

'Allow me to rephrase,' said Angela. 'It's not so much that I can't. It's that I won't.'

Julian stood with a baffled smile on his face.

'Sorry, Angela, I'm being a doddery old wotsit again,' he laughed. 'Catch a chap up?'

Angela put her hands on the table and rose slowly to her feet.

'As everyone on the committee will be aware,' she began, 'part of the role – indeed, responsibility – of our chair, is to ensure good management of our finances.'

'Ooooh, yes,' said Coral. 'We don't want another

fiasco like the Easter bake sale. I don't think Pauline from flat 35 ever got over that argument about what her Bakewell tart was worth. She can't so much as smell an almond without having a funny turn.'

'Well, quite,' said Angela, baring her teeth. 'And so, it saddens me to say, I simply cannot support Julian's appointment.'

There was a gasp from around the table as mouths dropped to the floor. Along with at least two pairs of teeth.

'But . . . but . . . why ever not, dear girl?' Julian stammered. 'You've been saying what a fine job you'd thought I'd do.'

'Ah, yes,' Angela sighed. 'But that was before . . . the subscriptions incident.'

'Oh dear,' said Peri from his mobility scooter. 'Did he sign up for one of those online dating sites? I was promised true love. All I got was spam about an energy-efficient boiler. Which I do also love, to be fair.'

'No, Peri,' Angela replied. 'I'm sorry to have to tell you that our new chair . . . has misappropriated the residents' subscriptions!'

Another gasp went up around the table.

'Huh?' Will asked Ani.

'It means he's been stealing money,' she said. 'But that doesn't sound like Julian. He's so honest he once came round to apologize for kicking our doormat out of place. After he'd put it back. This is absolute—'

'Angela!' Julian cried. 'Why on earth would you say such a thing? I would never dream . . . I haven't ever . . . I don't understand!'

'Just yesterday, I witnessed our chair-elect use some of the subscription money to finance his lunch,' Angela declared. 'I have been in torment ever since.'

'But . . . that's not what happened!' Ani whispered. 'We were there! She encouraged him to use that money! She's lying!'

Will was starting to see what the Shakespeareans meant about the power of stories. Angela was telling a tale. And in the wrong hands, they could be the most dangerous weapons of all.

'This is outrageous!' Julian cried. 'Angela, why would you do this?'

'All right, everyone,' said a man, standing up calmly. 'Clearly there has been some kind of misunderstanding. I'm sure we can clear it all up quickly enough. Julian – did you or didn't you use the subscription money to buy your lunch?'

In between two breaths, Julian seemed to change from a dignified elderly gentleman to a scared little boy.

'Well, Henry,' he began.

'It's Richard,' corrected one of the Kings.

'So sorry, Richard – it's not quite as simple as that,' he began.

'Oh, I think it is,' Angela scoffed. 'So tell us, Mr Chairman-elect. Did you or didn't you buy your lunch with the Arden Heights subscription money?'

Julian looked totally lost for words.

'I did,' he said quietly. 'But I can assure you that as soon as I went to the bank I immediately—'

But whatever he was going to say was lost in the furore as the committee erupted in outrage.

'What a load of old pony!' cried Richard King.

'It's an outrage!' Coral agreed.

'Has anyone seen my teeth?' Peri mumbled.

'Please, wait, you don't understand,' Julian pleaded over the angry voices. 'It's just a simple misunderstanding, I can explain . . .'

But no one wanted to listen.

'If I may,' Angela cut over the furore. 'I refer you to the rules of this committee. In the event of the chair being found unfit or unable to carry out their duties, protocol dictates that leadership passes to the deputy chair. Which just happens . . . to be me.'

Will watched Julian's sad eyes lock on to his 'friend'. He realized what was going on here. And so did Will.

'You, Angela?' he said quietly. 'You?'

Angela looked back into his despairing face.

'Yes, Julian,' she said coldly. 'Me. All in favour.'

Every hand around the table crept up. Julian hung his head. Angela nodded hers in satisfaction.

'Then, as your chair, I call this meeting to order,' Angela said sternly. 'And I must insist that anyone not on the committee leave the room. Immediately.'

Will could feel himself getting angry. This wasn't fair. Angela had twisted the truth of what happened until it barely resembled the facts. And yet she'd said nothing untrue. That was evil. Seriously evil.

But if Will was getting upset, he had nothing on Ani.

'This . . . this . . . this is outrageous!' she raged, storming into the room, to everyone's surprise. And to Will's own surprise, he found himself following her. 'That isn't what happened – we were there!'

'Julian didn't do anything wrong,' Will added, feeling a heat rise from his belly to his voice. 'Angela's . . . Angela is lying.'

The collective gasp sucked the air out of the room. Will could feel Ani looking at him. She too was surprised. But was that also pride in her eyes?

'Well, now, my dears,' said Angela, her tone as cold and hard as stone. 'I don't know what little trick you think you're playing. But the grown-ups are talking.'

'Yeah, they're talking,' Ani spat. 'They're talking complete—'

'Nonsense,' Will interrupted before Ani could get them into even more trouble. 'Julian hasn't done anything! And you're all supposed to be his friends! You know him! Why won't you believe him?'

Some of the committee had the decency to look at least a bit embarrassed. But Angela merely kept her steely gaze.

'I had a feeling we were going to have trouble from you two the moment I laid eyes on you,' she said. 'Now, no one is going to believe your naughty fibs.'

'They're not fibs!' Ani raged. 'We were there, we heard what happened.'

'I will be speaking to both of your parents,' said Angela firmly. 'And thank you for reminding me of one of my first orders of business. Arden Heights was designed to be a community for senior citizens. Children are delightful, of course. But you are also noisy and bothersome. I suggest we amend the constitution to ban children from overnight stays.'

'Wait, you can't do that!' Ani roared. 'We're here to look after Olivia! It's just me and Ben! We moved out of our house to come here!'

Not for the first time, Will was confused. Ani said she was staying temporarily with Ben. Where had 'our house' come from?

'Then you need to make up your mind, sweetie,'

Angela said with a smile that could cut glass. 'Do you want to come here telling your tall tales? Or do you want to go back to your flat with your family, where you belong?'

Will could see the words fighting to come out of Ani's mouth. But he also knew how much she cared about Olivia. So somehow, with a great struggle, she swallowed them back down.

'There now,' smiled Angela triumphantly. 'As I was saying. This is a residents' committee meeting. Therefore I must insist that all non-members leave. Right. Now.'

Will watched Julian try to hold his head up as he walked past his supposed friends on what now seemed like the longest walk out of the recreation room. And he could see the tears in Julian's eyes as he did it.

'Children?' Angela said, with daggers in her stare. 'Run along. We have work to do.'

Will looked to Ani, who still seemed ready to fight. But they'd lost this battle. It was time to retreat.

They turned around and walked back into the lift. They rode back up in silence, a tiring day starting to take its toll.

'I left my stuff at yours,' Ani said eventually. 'Can I grab it before I go home?'

'Of course,' said Will. 'And, hey, I thought what you did in there was . . . kinda cool.'

Ani smiled a weak smile.

'You were kinda cool too,' she said as the lift doors opened on to their floor and they walked towards Will's open flat door. 'It was good to hear you speak up. Let's get some sleep and see how it all looks tomorr—'

But before she could finish her sentence, she was stopped by two things. One was the two new arrivals in Will's flat. And the other was the look of horror on Will's face.

'William,' came the clipped tones of Uncle Claude. 'Jon and I thought we'd pay you a little visit. Now do get the kettle on. We're absolutely parched.'

CHAPTER XIV

Two Ignoble Kinsmen

'What are you doing here?' were the first words Will could form. His stay at Arden Heights hadn't exactly been relaxing. But at least it hadn't included Claude and Jon.

'Come on, Will,' said Mary, rushing up behind Claude. 'That's no way to greet your uncle and cousin.' Will looked at his mum. It was as though she'd changed shape – she was somehow smaller, somehow less. And the light that had been slowly reigniting in her eyes?

It had been extinguished again.

'Missed me, Rat?' whispered Jon, his mean eyes matching his mean smile.

'I'm sure he has,' Uncle Claude said slickly. 'And who do we have here?'

'Ani,' said Will's friend bluntly. He could feel her gaze

on him. But he couldn't return it. His would give too much away.

'A woman of few words,' Claude replied with an unpleasant smirk. 'What a rare treat. Mary!'

Will could feel his teeth clench at the barked command.

'Yes?' his mum said wearily.

'We've had a long journey. Take our bags to our rooms,' Claude instructed.

Mary looked between the two bedrooms.

'But . . . there are only two rooms,' she said. 'Will and I are using them.'

'Not any more you're not,' said Claude. 'We'll sleep after dinner. Which will be what?'

'I, um . . . I don't know,' Mary said, reaching for Claude's large suitcase. 'I wasn't expecting you. I didn't get anything in.'

Will watched Claude roll his eyes and open his wallet. He dropped some twenty-pound notes on the floor.

'Then sort it out,' he said, heading for the front room. 'And, Will, fetch me that drink. The train ride was frightful. First class isn't nearly what it used to be. They didn't even provide basic refreshments.'

'Did they provide some basic manners?' Ani chipped in. 'Because you don't seem to have brought those either.'

Uncle Claude stopped, turned slowly and started to

walk back towards Ani. Will winced.

'I. Beg. Your. Pardon?' he said, flecks of spit accompanying each word.

'Ani, why don't you go home, love?' said Mary softly. 'We'll see you tomorrow.'

'Nice girlfriend you've got there, Rat,' Jon whispered in Will's ear. 'Must be fun to have someone to play dollies with.'

Will refused to wince as Jon's foot pressed down hard on his. He wasn't going to show him it hurt. That just encouraged him.

'I said,' Ani spelt out, apparently not even slightly intimidated by Uncle Claude, 'that you need to find some manners, you ignorant, obnoxious—'

'There you are!' came Ben's voice behind her. 'I've been looking for you – dinner's getting . . .'

A single glance around the tense gathering was all Ben needed to read the room.

'Oh, I'm sorry – I'm interrupting,' he said awkwardly.

'Not at all,' Mary said nervously. 'Everyone, this is our neighbour, Ben. Ben, this is my brother Claude and nephew Jon.'

'Pleased to meet you,' said Ben politely. Claude sneered in response.

'I was just about to reprimand your daughter,' Claude responded, his angry eyes not leaving Ani's defiant ones.

'It would appear that someone needs to.'

Will watched Ben's hackles rise. Ben looked at Ani, who gave him a reassuring little smile, before putting a protective hand on Ani's shoulder. Will felt the familiar pang of missing his dad. Leo would never have let Uncle Claude speak to him like that either.

'If there is any disciplining to be done, I'll be taking care of it myself,' said Ben coldly. 'For whoever needs it.'

Ben, a much bigger man than Uncle Claude, pulled himself up to his full height to make his meaning very clear. Uncle Claude seemed to understand. Ben turned his gaze to Mary, his face softening with pity.

'Is there anything I can do to help?' he asked. 'You appear to have your hands full.'

'And my flat,' said Mary with a weak smile.

'I think you'll find it's *my* flat,' said Uncle Claude with a self-satisfied smile. 'Like everything else Father owned. He left it to me. And I have his will to prove it.'

Will watched Mary bite her tongue, as he'd been watching her do for the past two years. It was a miracle she hadn't bitten it off by now.

'We have a slight accommodation shortage,' she said. 'I can sleep on the sofa.'

'Or he can,' said Ani, gesturing to Jon. 'You're not seriously going to let your aunt sleep on the couch? You're just a kid.'

'And you're just a nobody,' Jon said, his finger extending to jab Ani on the shoulder. 'So why don't you mind your own—'

It happened so quickly, Will barely had time to process it. Before Jon could make contact with Ani's shoulder, his wrist was firmly in Ben's grasp.

'Allow me to be very clear, young man,' Ben growled. 'If you lay one finger – one fingernail – on her, you will be dealing with me. Do. You. Understand?'

'Oh, come, come, now,' said Uncle Claude with fake joviality. 'Children will be children, will they not? Just roughhousing.'

'Yeah,' said Jon, pinching Will's hip hard. 'Just roughhousing.'

'Well, roughhouse somewhere else,' said Ben. 'Will can stay with us, Mary. Ani has bunk beds, it's no problem.'

Will watched his mum's face almost break with gratitude.

'Thank you,' she said. 'That's very kind of you, Ben.'

'And you?' Ben asked gently. 'Will you be all right?'

Mary forced a smile.

'I'll be fine,' she said. 'It's just like being at home.'

Will's stomach lurched at her words. That was the very last thing either of them needed.

'Go and get your things,' Ben said to Will. 'And bring your appetite. We always order too much pizza.'

Will smiled and headed for his room.

'I'll take this, Aunty Mary,' said Jon, reaching for his bag. 'Save you the trouble.'

Will tried to find the words to object. But he was tired. And he knew it would be quicker and easier just to let it all play out.

'Thanks,' said Will's mum suspiciously. 'Appreciate it.'

'No trouble,' said Jon, walking into the bedroom behind Will and shutting the door. 'Won't be long.'

'You OK?' Ani asked half an hour later as she tucked into her umpteenth slice of pizza. 'Not hungry?'

'We can order something else if you'd prefer,' Ben said. 'Or I can make you something?'

Will smiled at his hosts.

'Thank you. Really,' he said. 'I'm just not very hungry tonight.'

He could feel Ben's eyes on him. But he didn't want to look back.

'Snooze you lose,' said Ani, snatching his slice of pepperoni off his plate. 'So what's the deal with Claude and Jon? Why are they such buttheads?'

'Ani Hathaway,' Ben chided. 'How many times do we need to have the conversation about inside thoughts and outside thoughts?'

Ani shrugged.

'At least once more,' she said through a mouth of pizza. 'So, Will? What gives?'

Will sighed and pushed his plate away.

'I dunno,' he said. 'It's like . . . it's like my uncle didn't want to look bad by not taking my mum in after my dad died. But he didn't actually want to do it. And he needs us to know that. Every day.'

There was a silence around the table.

'I liked your grandfather very much,' Ben said eventually. 'He and my mum were great friends. I didn't get to know Rex well, but every time I met him I was struck by what a gentleman he was.'

Will couldn't help but scoff.

'Tell that to my mum,' he said quietly. 'He wasn't much of a gentleman with her. He ditched her when she moved in with my dad.'

Ben looked at him sympathetically.

'Families are very complicated machines,' he said kindly. 'We know all about that.'

'Amen,' said Ani, reaching for the dough balls.

'Is Mary . . . is your mum OK, though? Ben asked. 'I mean, Claude's all right to her?'

'He's given us a home and he's given her a job,' Will trotted out, as his uncle had said to him so many times before. 'And she's grateful for that. Mainly because she doesn't have any other choice.'

Ben shook his head.

'I'm sorry to hear that Rex didn't ensure she had more choices,' he said quietly.

'So am I,' came Will's even quieter reply.

'So,' Ben began carefully. 'You two have been busy, I hear. Angela paid me a visit this evening. She told me what you did at the meeting.'

Ani and Will exchanged worried looks. Were they in trouble?

Ben leant forward over the table.

'Well done, both of you,' he winked. 'She should be ashamed of herself, stabbing Julian in the back like that, and I told her so. Good on you both for standing up to it.'

Will watched as Ben stroked Ani's cheek proudly. He felt the deep ache for his dad. Life would be so different if he'd been allowed to keep him. He stifled a small yawn. It had been a really long day.

'Come on,' said Ben, putting a friendly hand on Will's shoulder. 'Let's get you pair settled. Lord knows what you've got planned for tomorrow.'

'We're going to win the vote, that's what we've got planned,' said Ani determinedly. 'Aren't we, Will?'

'If you say so.' Will yawned openly this time. He wasn't sure about anything any more. Except the fact that he really needed some sleep.

'I do,' said Ani brightly. She leant in to whisper to him. 'And don't worry. We've got all night to figure it out. Ben sleeps like a log, he'll never hear us chatting . . .'

Thirty minutes later, the only sound to fill Ani's bedroom was the sound of her snoring. She had conked out the minute her head hit the pillow and was now in a deep slumber. But despite his bone-tiredness, Will couldn't get to sleep. His brain and body were full of sensation, every time he tossed or turned, a new one prickling at his soul or skin. Ben had given him a glass of water, but in the warmth of the night he'd already drunk it all. His mouth was as dry as sand, so he got up, softly walked out of the bedroom and found the kitchen effortlessly in the dark, his internal compass treading the same path he did in his own flat.

Will turned on the tap, filled his glass and drank it, before refilling it again. He was about to return to the bedroom, when a soft voice in the doorway stopped him.

'Rex,' said Olivia, her loose white hair flowing down her shoulders. 'Good to see you, my friend. Come. Come and sit with me. Tell me your stories.'

Will wasn't sure what to do. But then he remembered what Ani had said about going along with it. And it wasn't like he could sleep anyway.

He followed Olivia through to the front room and sat with her at the dining-room table. Her face was shining in the moonlight, illuminating her white hair like a halo around her head. She stared into his face.

'You look troubled,' she said. 'Is it Mary? Are you worrying about her? I know you worry so.'

Will looked into Olivia's kind eyes.

'Yeah,' he said. 'Yeah, I really am.'

Olivia reached for his hand over the table.

'You've taken care of her,' she said. 'She's going to be all right. Just you see. You love her. She knows that.'

Will could feel the tears coming to his eyes. He knew that Olivia didn't know what she was saying. But he still wished it was true. Rex wasn't taking care of his mum. No one was.

'Oh, Rex,' she said, handing Will a clean hankie. 'So many tears. Let me hold some of them for you. Tell me what's troubling you.'

Will looked into Olivia's kind, caring face. He hadn't been able to tell anyone what was troubling him. He couldn't. It would cause too much trouble. He couldn't even tell his own mother. But he needed to tell someone. It had been eating away at him for months. Will hadn't been able to tell a living soul.

So he took a deep breath.

And he told Olivia his story.

CHAPTER XV

Much Ado About Something

'This place is an absolute tip!' Uncle Claude declared the next day, while doing precisely nothing to fix it. 'Get it sorted. Jon and I are going out for the day. The developers won't want to waste any time once this vote passes tonight. Keep anything of any value and toss the rubbish in a skip.'

'In you get, then,' Will heard his mum mutter under her breath as they worked their way through the last stacks of papers.

Ani giggled as she sorted out a pile of receipts.

'See you, loser,' whispered Jon, accidentally on purpose kicking Will on his way out of the door.

'I've got an idea for you,' Ani said sweetly to Uncle Claude.

'What?' said Claude sharply.

'You see the pier down there?' said Ani, pointing out of the window.

'What of it?' he snapped.

'It's quite short,' said Ani innocently. 'But it's great for a long walk.'

Will heard Mary snort into her sorting. Uncle Claude's eyes narrowed.

'You are an insolent little brat,' Claude spat.

'Probably,' Ani whispered. 'But I dare you to say that to Ben. I could call out for him now . . . BEN!'

Will watched Uncle Claude recoil.

'Come along, Jon,' he said hastily. 'We have reservations at The Royale for lunch.'

'Don't choke on it, will you?' said Ani with a saccharine smile as they scuttled out of the flat.

'It's very kind of you to come and help,' Mary said gratefully. 'But you really don't have to be here.'

Ani shrugged.

'No biggie,' she said. 'I've got nothing better to do. And, honestly, it's taking my mind off the vote tonight.'

'I think it's wonderful how hard you've worked to try to save the Heights,' Mary said, touching Ani's arm proudly. 'This place is . . . complicated for me. But I so hope it goes your way. You deserve it. I wish I could help, but . . .'

'Claude,' Ani sighed. 'I understand. It's not your fault.

But if we've persuaded at least some people to vote against . . . We just have to hope.'

'Everything OK?' panted Ben, running into the flat. 'Ani, I heard you shout out, are you— Oh. Hi. Mary.'

Will watched as his mum hastily pulled her hair out of . . . whatever it was that was holding her hair up. She stood up and straightened her T-shirt and jeans, which made precisely no difference to the crumpled, dusty mess she was. He couldn't believe it. His mum . . . his mum was actually blushing.

Adults were so, so weird.

'Ah, hi, Ben,' she said nervously. 'What can . . . how . . . why . . . um . . .'

'I'm sorry to barge in,' said Ben, running an anxious hand through his dark hair. 'I heard Ani yell and so . . .'

'I'm fine,' Ani beamed, looking between Ben and Will's mum. 'Claude was just being an idiot.'

'Ani,' her father chided. 'That's no way to talk about Mary's brother.'

'Oh, it's exactly the way to talk about Mary's brother,' Will's mum smiled. 'I wish more people did.'

She laughed nervously and Ben joined her. Will couldn't believe what he was seeing. It was like when Troy asked Cass out to the Year Nine Prom and ended up being sick on her rucksack.

Only this was way, way more embarrassing.

'Wow,' said Ben, looking around the war zone of paperwork around them. 'You really do have your work cut out for you, don't you?'

'You have no idea,' Mary groaned. 'My father was compiling his life story and kept copies of absolutely everything. So I don't know whether I'm going to find the answer to eternal youth or a receipt from Aldi.'

'Well, you don't need the first one,' Ben replied, looking just like Troy did before he puked. 'Sorry, I just meant that you . . . you look so . . . I wasn't trying to . . .'

'Smooth, Ben,' Ani groaned with a whisper. 'Real smooth.'

'Cooee!' came a high-pitched whine at the door. 'Can I come in?'

There was a collective moan at the sound of Angela's voice.

'Do we have a choice?' Ani replied.

'Hello, my dears,' said Angela, glaring at Ani as though she were mould. 'I just wanted to pop by to remind everyone about the vote tonight – and to drop by the new code of conduct rules for Arden Heights. Make sure we're all on the same page.'

She handed thick booklets to Mary and Ben.

'Wow,' said Mary, flicking through the many pages. 'This is . . . comprehensive.'

'And, er, legally dubious,' said Ben, squinting at a page.

'You can't ban people from humming, Angela.'

'Or from playing music post-1975, I would imagine,' Mary added.

'Oh, come on!' Ben exclaimed. 'There's no way you can stop people from wearing denim. Angela, this is ridiculous.'

'I'm just trying to create an environment everyone can enjoy,' said Angela unapologetically.

'Not if you like to hum Taylor Swift in your jeans, you're not,' Mary muttered, making Ben laugh out loud. 'You can't seriously expect people to adhere to this, Angela. It's . . . it's despotic.'

Will didn't know what that word meant. But he knew Angela didn't like it.

'Well, of course, everyone is free to interpret the new rules how they wish,' she said. 'Just like the residents' committee is free to decide when leases are renewed . . .'

'You can't kick people out for not agreeing to your ridiculous rules,' said Ben more forcefully. 'Not on my watch. I would personally challenge the legality of that.'

Will had to admit it, Ben was pretty impressive when he was fired up. And, judging by his mother's wide-eyed smile, he wasn't alone in thinking so.

'Classy, Mum,' he whispered to his gawping mother. 'Keeping it really classy.'

Mary snapped her jaw shut immediately.

'Well, as you can see, Angela, we have a lot to do. Thanks for popping round.'

She gestured towards the door in an unequivocal invitation to leave.

'Always a pleasure,' Angela said with a smile that could open a tin.

'So that just happened,' Ben said, tossing the booklet away. 'Look, Mary – I've taken some time off today for madam here to completely ignore me, so I'm at a loose end. I could help, if you like? I mean, I'm a lawyer, so I'm largely useless at most things. But paperwork I understand.'

'Oh, no,' said Mary, rearranging her fringe. 'I couldn't possibly.'

'Great, you can start over there,' Ani directed, pointing Ben towards a large pile of . . . something near Mary. Will inched towards her.

'What are you doing?' he whispered to her.

'Just helping them along,' said Ani with a mischievous smile. 'You know what adults are like. Sometimes you have to point them in the right direction.'

'And you think getting those two together is the right direction?' he replied sceptically. 'More like a diversion off a cliff.'

Will hadn't really thought about his mum being with someone else. She and Dad were so in love, he'd never imagined there'd be any space left.

'You think, huh?' said Ani, gesturing to where Ben and Mary were giggling over something she'd found amongst the paper debris.

'Why would anyone keep fifty years of dentist appointments?!' Mary laughed. 'My dad had false teeth!'

As Will saw his mum lit up and smiling, he realized that he'd like to see her happy again. No one could replace his dad. But maybe someone could rebuild Mary's smile. And he was OK with that.

They all worked together in a cloud of happy chatter for the next hour or so, Will noticing how much faster they were working through everything with Ani and Ben's help. He wasn't the only grateful one – Ben's legal expertise was incredibly useful for his mum in deciding what was important to keep and what was on a one-way ticket to the skip. After another stint of hard work, Mary stood up with a grunt, holding her back.

'Come on, everyone,' she said. 'Time for a break. I'll make us all a cuppa. Oh, no. That's right. Jon used the last of the milk on the last of the cereal this morning. Then left both on the side. Sorry.'

'Oh . . . well, have you been to the new cafe in town?' Ben offered. 'They do the most amazing Columbian blend – if you like that sort of thing.'

'Are you kidding me?' Mary yelped. 'I would sell my

grandmother for a decent cup of coffee . . . sorry, Granny.'

She blew a kiss to a picture of Will's great-grandmother on Rex's desk.

'Well, I promise not to keep the receipt,' Ben said, making Mary laugh. She was relaxed again, Will noticed, her face not carrying the strain of last night. 'So, if you'd like to . . . we could head there now. Take a stroll along the front – maybe even treat ourselves to a muffin?'

'Sold!' Mary shouted. 'For a muffin, frankly I'd marry you . . . Oh – I didn't mean . . . I was only kidding, I . . .'

'I know,' said Ben with a smile. 'Er, kids? Do you want to join us? I mean, we'll probably just be talking about boring grown-up stuff, but you're . . . welcome to join us.'

Ani shot Will daggers, but she didn't need to. One look at his mother's face told him he had never been less welcome to join anything in his life.

'We're fine here,' he said. 'I really want to finish *2000*.'

'Yeah,' said Ani. 'You two run along. And don't get into too much mischief, will you?'

Mary blushed again. Ben smiled shyly.

'Well, come on, then,' he said, offering his hand to help her over the stacks of paper all around her.

'Thank you,' said Mary, accepting his help to negotiate the paper maze. 'We won't be long, kids. Behave.'

'You too,' said Will, earning him a hair ruffle as Mary

walked past him.

'That's going to be an interesting story,' said Ani as Ben stood back to allow Mary out of the flat.

'Let's just hope it doesn't end in tragedy,' said Will, moving the folder he'd been sorting off the pile to start on the next one.

But as its title was revealed, the name on the front jumped out at him:

BIANCA MINOLA

Will felt his heart quicken. Why did Rex have a file on Ms Minola's daughter? He opened it with trembling fingers, not sure he wanted to know what was inside.

'What's that?' said Ani, turning her head upside down to read the label on the file. 'Oh, wow, is it . . . ?'

'Yeah,' said Will grimly, skipping through the pages of handwritten notes and copies of documents. 'Looks like Ms Minola wasn't the only one trying to find Bianca.'

'Well, what does it say?' Ani practically squealed.

Will skipped through to the final page in the folder. If the week had taught him anything, it was that his grandfather kept everything in meticulous order. The answer would be at the end of the file . . .

And there it was.

'Oh, no,' he said softly as he read the last entry. He grabbed Ani's hand to help her off the floor.

‘Come on. We have to get to Ms Minola,’ he urged. ‘Now.’

‘She won’t want to see us,’ Ani insisted. ‘You heard her. Her daughter is coming today.’

Will handed the terrible piece of paper over to his friend.

‘No, she’s not,’ he said quietly. ‘Because Bianca Minola died twenty-five years ago.’

CHAPTER XVI

Love's Labour's Lost

They raced to the lift and were about to give up for the stairs, when the doors pinged open.

'So if Bianca isn't alive,' Ani asked, 'who is that with Ms Minola?'

'I don't know,' Will said grimly. 'But we need to tell her what Rex found. What the . . .'

As they stepped into the lift, they saw it was plastered with rules from the new code of conduct, signed off by Angela. New rules about labelling bins, banning ball games in the pool, telling them that rap music would be reported to the police. They were everywhere.

'Wow,' said Ani. 'Might have to go to prison for a holiday. It'll be more fun than here. Looks like the power has gone to someone's head.'

'D'ya think?' said Will, pointing to a notice banning

dogs over a certain width. 'Angela's lost the plot.'

'And will lose us a load of against votes if this is the world she's creating here,' Ani groaned. 'Who's going to want to stay at Arden Heights if this is how it's going to be? I could murder Lady M.'

But they didn't have time to dwell. The lift arrived at the ground floor and they sprinted to Ms Minola's door. Only this time, there wasn't an orchestra of locks to get through. The door was wide open.

'Oh, no,' said Will. 'Do you think we should go and get . . .'

But Ani was already racing inside.

'Ms Minola!' she cried out. 'Ms Minola? Are you—'

Her question was answered immediately as Will ran in behind her. Ms Minola was OK – physically at least. But her flat was not. Every drawer and cupboard had been opened and tipped out. The place was a mess.

Its owner was sitting in the middle of it, surrounded by groceries and staring blankly around the wasteland.

'What happened?' Ani asked softly, crouching down to the woman staring at the floor.

'She told me she loved roast chicken,' Ms Minola said quietly. 'And I wanted to cook my little girl a meal. And I wanted it to be her favourite. But when I came back from the shops . . .'

Ms Minola gestured around the disaster.

'Has she taken anything?' Will asked. 'We should call the police.'

'Some money. A ring. A necklace. A bracelet,' said Ms Minola sadly. 'But no police. I don't want any more fuss.'

Will didn't know what to do. Ms Minola looked . . . so defeated. Ani put her hand on her neighbour's.

'Ms Minola,' she began. 'I'm so, so sorry. This is all my fault, I should never have . . .'

A lined hand rested on top of her young friend's.

'The only person at fault here is me,' she said. 'There is no fool like an old fool. She didn't even look like her picture, but I didn't want to see it. You tried to warn me. I didn't want to listen.'

Ani looked around the flat.

'Look, we can help,' she said, starting to pick some things up. 'We'll tidy up for you, get everything back to how it was.'

'Leave it,' said Ms Minola, shaking her head. 'The new owners can sort it all out. I just want to get as far away from here as possible.'

Will waited for Ani to argue with her. To tell her how important it was that she voted against. To try to change her mind.

But she simply put her arms around Ms Minola's shoulders.

'I understand,' she whispered in her ear. 'I'm so sorry

this happened to you.'

Will found himself swallowing a lump in his throat. He desperately wanted to do something to help. He looked down. The file from Rex's study was trembling in his hands. He offered it to Ms Minola.

'Here,' he said. 'My grandfather looked for Bianca too. I don't know how to tell you . . .'

Ms Minola looked down at the file, but didn't take it. She closed her eyes.

'She's gone, isn't she?' she whispered.

Will couldn't think of any better answer than the truth.

'She has,' he said quietly. 'I'm so sorry.'

Ms Minola nodded resignedly.

'I knew it,' she said softly. 'On some level I've always known it. I can't feel her. And I'd know if she was walking this earth. She's part of me. And she's lost.'

Will watched Ani wipe a tear from her cheek. This was not how either of them had wanted this story to end.

'I don't know if this helps,' said Will hesitantly, not wanting to make the situation worse. 'But she's here. In St Crispin's churchyard. Rex found her grave.'

He pulled the page out of the file and handed it over. Ms Minola choked back a tear and traced her fingers over the unfamiliar name on the gravestone.

'Would . . . would you like to go and see her?' Ani

offered. 'Ben will take us. His dad is there too, we often go and put flowers on his grave. We could go today? You said it's her birthday?'

Ms Minola's dewy eyes looked at her young friends.

'It is. And I'd like that very much,' she said. 'Thank you, children. But for now I need a moment alone.'

'Of course,' said Will, leaving the folder on the table. 'I'll leave this here. It belongs to you.'

Ms Minola nodded a wordless thanks. Ani gave her another hug, then they gently backed out of the room and her flat.

'That's so horrible,' Ani said, her voice wavering as they walked back towards the lift. 'Parents and their children . . . that shouldn't happen.'

'Yeah,' sighed Will. Losing his dad had been incredibly hard. But at least he'd got to have him for a while. Ms Minola had been denied even that. Life, as well he knew, could be so incredibly unfair.

'Oh, hi, Rosie,' said Ani as the gardener walked towards them. 'How – er – how are you feeling today?'

'Fine,' said Rosie quickly, looking embarrassed. 'I'm off to view a new flat. It's a couple of hours away from here, I need a change of scene.'

She stopped dead as she met Patrick coming the other way.

'Rosie?' he said softly. 'Why don't you come in for a

cuppa and a chat?'

'No, thank you,' said Rosie sharply. 'I . . . I have to go.'

'Rosie, wait,' Patrick called after her. But it was no use. Rosie couldn't get away fast enough.

Patrick sighed.

'I was going to plan the autumn planting,' he said sadly. 'Now I don't know if any of us will be here to see it.'

'Patrick,' Ani began. But he had already shuffled off down the hall towards his flat.

Will and Ani walked to the lift and stood there in silence. What more was there to say?

The lift doors opened to reveal two unfamiliar women inside. Will figured from their ages – they were more like his mum's age – that they weren't Arden Heights residents. Ani smiled at them, but they didn't acknowledge her. They were deep in conversation.

'I'm telling you, that sideboard would look horrible in your front room,' the dark-haired woman said to the blonde. 'It doesn't match your sofa. Much better *I* get it.'

'No way,' the other woman pouted. 'Mum always said it was mine. You can have Mum and Dad's bed.'

'Why would I want that?' the other woman – her sister, Will deduced – scoffed. 'They've had that since they were married. It's ancient.'

'Look, I'm the one who's going to be stuck with him,'

the first sister proclaimed. 'So it's only fair I get first dibs on the furniture.'

'Would you rather pay nursing home fees?' the blonde-haired woman protested. 'My neighbour put her mum in a home last year, they had to sell the house by Christmas, couldn't afford it.'

'We're agreed on that,' said Sister One. 'But I still get the sideboard.'

'Georgia?' Ani asked, putting the pieces together just before Will could. 'And Regina?'

'Who's asking?' Georgia said waspishly.

'We're friends of Monty's, of your dad's,' Will said. 'We're just on our way to see him.'

'Come to say goodbye, have you?' Regina said airily.

'Goodbye? No,' Ani insisted. 'Why would we do that?'

'Because the stubborn old goat has finally agreed to sell this place and move in with me,' Georgia said.

'Since when?' Ani exclaimed.

'Since last night,' Regina sighed. 'The timing's terrible, of course. I had a spa day booked and everything. Thank goodness for the cruise I'm booking with my share of the sale, I'll need a holiday after all the stress.'

'Wait, Monty's selling his flat . . . and you're keeping the money?' Ani raged, despite an attempt at a calming nudge from Will.

'Not that it is any of your business,' Georgia said

grandly, 'but he's getting a roof over his head, food in his belly, clothes, medical expenses. It's the least we are owed.'

'He's your dad,' Ani said darkly. 'It's you who owe him.'

The lift doors opened and Ani didn't even wait for them to fully part before she was pelting down the hallway.

'Ani, wait!' Will called after her, running to catch up, but unable to match her speed or her head start.

'Monty!' Ani cried, knocking on her door. 'Monty! You can't go! Not like this! Not with them! Monty! Open up!'

'*Bambina!*' the soothing voice came as the door opened. 'Calm yourself! Everything is *bene*!'

'You're not going?' Will panted, finally catching up. Monty's kind blue eyes crinkled all over.

'*Sì*,' he said gently. 'It is time, my friend. There is no life for me at Arden Heights. My future is with my girls.'

'Papa!' came Georgia's sickly-sweet voice behind them. 'We're so excited you've changed your mind! We can't wait to spoil you rotten!'

'It's going to be like when we were kids!' Regina chimed in. 'The whole family back together again!'

'Monty, don't listen to them!' Ani gabbled breathlessly. 'They're going to stick you in some annexe and sell all your furniture and use your money to go on stupid cruises! Stay here! Stay with us! We can take care of you.'

'*Bambina!*' Monty laughed, cupping her face. 'You are

a good girl. But so are my girls! And it's their job to take care of me, not yours.'

'Our *privilege*,' Georgia mewed. 'Isn't it, Reggie?'

'Such a privilege,' said her sister through lips that could strain peas.

'So you see?' said Monty, raising his hands up again. 'Monty is looked after! All is well.'

'But . . . but . . . but . . . Arden Heights?' Ani protested weakly. Will watched her visibly wilt. And he got it. They were losing votes. Too many votes. Tonight was looking pretty grim.

Monty put his fingers beneath Ani's chin and lifted her eyes to his.

'I know you are disappointed, *bambina*,' he said gently. 'But we both make new homes. In new places. I promise you. You'll see.'

Ani nodded sadly. For once, she was all out of words.

'Come on,' said Will. 'We'd better get back. Mum and Ben will be worrying.'

'Bye,' said Georgia dismissively, sweeping into the flat. 'Right, Reggie, you start in there, I'll get going in here. Now where did Mum keep her jewellery?'

Will smiled at Monty and guided Ani back to the lift. They ascended to their floor in silence and walked back to flat 29. The sound of Mary and Ben's laughter filled the hallway as they walked inside.

'Well, there you are. We were about to call out the search party!' Ben said with a smile. 'What have you been up to?'

'Nothing,' Ani grumbled, kicking her left sandal with her right.

'Everything OK?' Mary asked, shooting Will a concerned look.

'Sure,' he shrugged.

'Ani,' said Ben, looking worried. 'Are you—'

'I need a swim,' said Ani. 'I'll catch you all later.'

She trudged out of the flat and Will felt the adult eyes land on him.

'What's that about?' Mary asked.

'Nothing,' said Will. There seemed little point in telling them what had happened – it would become clear enough at the vote that night. 'I-I'm just going to . . . get changed,' he said, heading for his room.

'Thank goodness for that!' Mary called after him. 'Those jeans are banned, didn't you hear?'

He left Ben and Mary laughing as he went to his room and ripped off his jumper – he was absolutely boiling. He was about to dig out another jumper when the conversation between his mum and Ben drew his ear.

'Do you need to go after Ani?' his mum asked gently. 'She seemed pretty upset.'

'Sometimes she just needs to take a minute,' said Ben.

'Poor kid's had a tough time. She feels things very deeply.'

'She's a wonderful young woman,' said Mary admiringly. 'I bet you'll miss her when her mum comes back from her tour.'

'Comes back?' Ben asked. 'Oh, no. This again . . .'

'I'm so sorry,' Mary replied. 'I didn't mean to suggest that . . .'

'No, please, you've done nothing wrong,' Ben reassured her. 'It's Ani, she does this.'

'Does what?' Mary asked, her voice full of concern.

Ben sighed.

'Tells stories,' he said. 'I get it, sometimes it's easier to create the world we want, rather than confront the one we have. And her mum being a singer, or actress, or model travelling the world is certainly a great story.'

Will felt his mind whirring. He'd had so many questions about Ani's tales. Was he about to get the answers?

'Wait, are you saying it's not true?' Mary said quietly. 'Her mum's not on tour?'

'And I'm not Ben the Good Old Family Friend,' Ben sighed. 'I'm her foster carer.'

'Ohhhhhh,' said Mary, echoing Will's thoughts. 'That makes so much more sense. So where's her mother?'

Will heard another heavy sigh.

'No one knows,' he said quietly. 'Ani Hathaway was abandoned on the beach as a baby.'

CHAPTER XVII

The Changeling

Will's mind was a blur as he walked into his room. Why hadn't Ani told him the truth? He would have understood. He'd thought . . . he'd thought they were friends.

But then again, had he told her all his secrets?

So lost in his own thoughts was he, that Will wasn't entirely aware he'd opened the *Complete Works* again, until the four Shakespeareans appeared before him, all looking guilty as sin. They were in Ancient Rome, the Colosseum dominating the background as trickles of words ran from the Trevi Fountain. He felt a hot rage bubble up inside him. Will needed to be angry with someone. And the Shakespeareans were as good a target as any.

'I can't *believe* you lot,' he hissed. 'The trouble you've caused.'

'Now, Master Will, do not be hasty,' Puck said, summoning some paper butterflies. 'The magic has gone, but the cakes were tasty.'

'And I have another wonderful scheme to ensure Monty is with his Sylvie!' Juliet beamed. 'I just know true love will conquer all!'

'I sense a foul plot with Mistress Angela,' said Lady Macbeth. 'She is evil and cruel and heartless. This I understand.'

'What's the point?' Yorick moaned. 'We all know how this ends.'

'Enough!' Will said, as loudly as he dared. 'You have all made it so, so much worse! The gardening committee can't wait to get out of here! Monty's daughters are probably fighting over the family silver as we speak! And Angela has started her very own dictatorship! I hope you're pleased with yourselves – no one in their right minds would vote to stay at Arden Heights after what you've done!'

The Shakespeareans mumbled their apologies and looked at their feet, Juliet dragging her tiptoes along the page and making the words swirl.

'Truly, we are sorry, Master William,' she said. 'But we've started to make amends . . .'

'No!' said Will firmly. 'You've done enough! I can see why Rex never set you free – you're bad enough inside the book! I can't imagine how awful you'd be on the outside!'

Even within his rage, Will knew he was being harsh. But . . . Claude, Ms Minola, Rex – now Ani. He had enough complicated characters in his world.

'Peace, young Will, we're ever your friends,' said Puck softly. 'We want you to find how your story ends.'

'Well, I don't,' said Will, holding the covers between his hands. 'I should have taken this to the charity shop the first time I saw you!'

'Our methods may not have been to your liking,' said Lady Macbeth, 'but our intentions were pure. We are sworn to protect the Bard. Your home is under threat. We stepped in.'

'Sure,' Yorick chimed in. 'She didn't murder anyone.'

'And we only ever wanted to help you,' Juliet chimed in. 'Forgive us, Master Bard, we pray thee.'

'Well, you didn't help!' hissed Will, who was all out of forgiveness. 'All you care about is yourselves! You've ruined everything! And I never want to see you again!'

He slammed the covers of the book shut, trying to drown out the shouts seeping from the pages as he did.

'The. End,' he muttered, tossing the book in the box of books bound for the charity shop. He'd had enough. He was going to find Ani. He didn't care about Shakespeareans or stories of any of it. He was going to walk away and live his life.

No matter what the weighty feeling in his chest had to say about it.

Will followed his usual route through the gardens. And as usual, he ran into a member of the gardening committee.

'Hello there, young man,' said Antoine with a sad smile.

'Er, hi, Antoine,' he said distractedly. 'How are you this morning?'

'I'm grand, thank you, Will,' he replied, looking anything but. 'Had the strangest dream last night, though.'

'What are you doing?' Will asked, looking at the box of plants Antoine had dug up from the flower beds.

'Oh, just taking a few cuttings,' he said sadly. 'You know. For my new place.'

'Well, wait a minute,' said Will cheerily. 'We don't know how the vote will go tonight. You might not have to move.'

'Yes, I will,' said Antoine, looking sadly to where Patrick was snoozing on his balcony. 'I've found a lovely retirement village not an hour from here. Lovely gardens, though their hydrangeas need a right good pruning.'

'But so do ours,' said Will softly. And then added,

'Hydrangeas are flowers, right?'

'They are.' Antoine laughed gently before returning to his digging. 'You know, it's a funny thing, gardening. You think you're in control of it, but you've got no chance! It's all about nature – too much sun, too much rain, wrong soil, wrong insects – it's all out of your control.'

He glanced over to Patrick's balcony again.

'And some plants just won't take,' he continued. 'Don't matter how much you try to create the right conditions, how hard you love them, how long you wait for them, they're just not meant to be. It's not their time. So best move on to something that will flourish.'

Will looked at flat 14. Patrick was now awake and looking mournfully at his friend. And suddenly Will got it.

There had been a lot of drama in the gardening committee.

But Will finally understood where the real love story had been blossoming.

'I don't know much about gardening,' he began. 'We had a competition to grow sunflowers in Year Five. I managed to grow a small carrot.'

Antoine laughed his soft laugh.

'But I do know that you love . . . this garden,' said Will. 'And I think . . . the garden . . . would really miss you if you went. And if plants haven't grown because it's been the wrong time for them . . . maybe you should try again another time?'

Antoine stopped his digging and looked up at Will with his milky eyes.

'What if nothing blooms?' he whispered.

Will gestured to the orchestra of colour around them, surrounding them with so many of the flowers that Antoine had planted.

'It will,' he said with a reassuring smile. 'I really believe it will.'

He felt Antoine's hand on his.

'You're a lovely boy,' he said. 'I'm glad we met. I'll miss you.'

'Me too,' said Will and he really meant it. He'd only been at Arden Heights for a few days. But it already felt more like home than anywhere he'd known for years.

And he wasn't ready to leave it.

He found Ani where he always did – by the sea. But today, she wasn't in it. She was sitting on the shore, looking out over it. It would have made a great sketch, Ani looking out over the beach that had started her story. He realized that he'd hardly drawn while being at the Heights. Real life had kept him too busy. Will dropped down next to her on the sand.

'I really thought I could do it,' she said after a long pause. 'Thought I could change their minds. Thought I could make a difference. It was stupid.'

'It wasn't stupid,' Will began. 'And you have made a difference.'

'Not a good one,' Ani objected. 'I made it all worse. I should have just kept my big mouth shut.'

'No!' Will cried, louder than he meant to. 'You were right to speak up! You are right about everything! This is a special place! It should be saved! It's not fair – none of it is fair.'

He picked up a rock and threw it into the water. There was another lengthy silence.

'What was your dad like?' Ani asked him eventually.

Will felt the complicated blend of happy memories and aching pain whenever he called his father to mind.

'He was great,' he said. 'His name was Leo and he was a nurse. He met my mum when she fell out of a tree. Her friend at work had bet her she wouldn't climb it and she did.'

'Peak Mary,' Ani smiled.

'Used to be,' Will sighed. 'Anyway, Mum won the bet and got to the top of the tree, then fell out of it climbing back down and broke her wrist. My dad was the duty nurse at the hospital – and he said they fell in love there and then. Apparently Dad told her: "If you promise never to break your bones, I'll promise never to break your heart."'

'Oh, wow – that's kinda corny, Leo,' Ani laughed. 'But kinda cute.'

'That was my dad,' said Will. 'Kinda corny. Kinda cute. And he kept his promise. Right up until the day he didn't.'

Will allowed himself, for the first time in a long time, to think about the day he lost his father.

'It's time,' Mary had said, waking him up and wrapping him in a duvet to travel to the hospital. It was the longest and shortest car ride of Will's life. He was terrified of not getting there in time. And he was terrified of getting there at all.

Because he knew when he did, he would have to say goodbye.

'This isn't the end,' his dad had said, barely able to be heard over all the bleeping machines by his hospital bed. 'You just have to turn the page.'

Ani handed him a tissue.

'Here,' she said. 'It's clean. Mostly.'

Will smiled through his tears. He'd had to learn to do that a lot. And he had learnt that it was possible.

He thought very carefully before his next utterance.

'So,' he said gently. 'Tell me about your mum.'

Ani carried on looking out at forever. She dropped

her head. And with it, the act.

'I wish I could,' she said after an eternity. 'I don't know anything. I don't have any stories about her. I don't even know what my story is. Maybe that's why I make so many up.'

Will nodded. That made perfect sense. His stay at Arden Heights had taught him that he wasn't the only one who liked to draw the world as he wanted it.

'Ben wants to adopt me,' Ani announced.

'Well, that's great!' said Will, genuinely happy for her. 'He's awesome – and he obviously loves you.'

'I keep telling him no,' Ani said, her own voice quivering. 'Because there's a bit of me – and you'll probably think this is stupid – there's a bit of me that thinks that if I do this, if I make a new family with Ben . . . then it's the end of my family . . . with my mum.'

Will hadn't thought to bring tissues. He let Ani cry for a moment. Then handed hers back to her.

'It's clean,' he said. 'Mostly.'

It was a great relief to see that Ani could laugh through her tears too.

'For what it's worth,' he added. 'I don't think it would be the end. You'd just be turning the page.'

Ani's nose wrinkled. Will smiled. At least she was considering it. They sat there for a while, looking across the ocean. It wasn't an awkward silence. It was peaceful.

Like the white space between the comic-book panels. There was something about it that made the stories come off the page.

'Right,' Ani said after a few moments, her normal business-like tone resumed. 'We've got things to do. Up you get.'

She sprang up and brushed herself down, yanking Will off the ground. Once again, he was amazed by Ani's ability to switch emotional gear. They headed back towards the beach steps and started the ascent to Arden Heights.

'Oh, great,' Ani moaned as a familiar figure came into view halfway up the stairs. 'Yes, Caleb, we know, we're not running.'

The caretaker growled at them, before returning to sweeping the sand from the steps.

'I'll catch you up,' said Will, his heart hammering in his chest.

'Don't be long,' Ani instructed. 'I'll go and work on Mary and Ben for the ride to St Crispin's. And I'll win.'

'Never in doubt,' said Will, smiling at his friend as she scampered up the steps.

Will cautiously approached the irascible caretaker, his hand reaching into his pocket.

'Whaddya want?' Caleb barked at him. 'Can't you see I'm busy?'

Will thought about retreating, about keeping his mouth shut and minding his own business. But then he thought about all the people around Arden Heights who hadn't spoken up. Antoine and Patrick. Monty and Sylvie. His own grandfather.

He pulled Anthony's card out of his pocket.

'I just . . . I just wanted to say,' he started quietly. 'That I think you do a really great job keeping Arden Heights such a nice place to be. It can't be easy cleaning up after so many people. And they might not see it. Or appreciate it. But they can feel it. And that's thanks to you. You're the one who makes the Heights a really nice place to be. So thank you. From everyone. Whether they know it or not.'

Will tentatively handed Anthony's business card over to Caleb. The caretaker took it and squinted at it. When he read the name, his eyes widened. There was a long, scary pause.

'Where did you get this?' he asked. But not in his usual bark. In a softer, kinder tone.

'Anthony's in town,' said Will simply. 'He's sorry. And he wants his brother back.'

The caretaker's brush clattered to the floor. He stood, frozen to the spot for many moments.

'It's . . . it's too late,' he said eventually, trying to hand the card back. 'Too much has happened, it's too messy.'

'Maybe,' said Will. 'But like I say. You're really good at cleaning things up.'

He picked up the brush and handed it back to Caleb. He'd only said a few words. But they seemed to make their mark.

'Thank you, young man,' said the caretaker gently. 'That's very kind of you.'

Will nodded and carried on up the steps. A thought stopped him.

'Although, Caleb, I have to know,' he said, turning back to the caretaker. 'Did you really used to write poetry?'

The caretaker turned to him, his face breaking into a hundred smiles.

'Clear off,' he said with a wink.

CHAPTER XVIII

Alas, Poor Bianca

Given what a good mood their parents were in, it didn't take much for Ani to persuade them to take Ms Minola to the churchyard.

'I really should visit my dad,' Ben said.

'Me too,' Mary agreed, although Will noticed she sounded considerably less sure. Uncle Claude hadn't allowed them to go to Rex's funeral. Will could hardly bear to think of his own father's – it had been so hard. But also so important – it was a chance to say goodbye. His mum had never had that with her father. That must have been even harder.

With Mary's car still at Doug's garage, Ben offered to drive everyone in his seven-seater, so at four p.m., they collected Ms Minola from her flat and, bunches of flowers in hand, made the short drive to the local church.

It was a silent journey, everyone a little lost in their own thoughts. Will knew his mum would be thinking of Rex, and Ben of his father. Ani was taking the likely outcome of the vote incredibly hard and it was clearly still weighing on her mind – although Will now understood how many other heavy thoughts she was carrying alongside it. He couldn't begin to imagine how Ms Minola felt about this saddest of journeys. And his own mind was such a beehive, he could barely think for the buzzing in his brain.

They pulled up outside St Crispin's, a very small, very old ivy-covered church that looked like it belonged in a storybook. There had been a wedding there recently, pieces of coloured confetti festooning the ground, their joyful colour clashing oddly with the sad grey of the nearby gravestones. Will considered that churches hosted the very best days of people's lives, and the very worst. Once again, he pushed the memory of his own father's funeral out of his mind. That had been the very worst day of his life. He was still waiting for the very best.

They stood at the entrance to the churchyard, each with a family member to visit.

'Is twenty minutes OK for everyone?' Ben asked quietly. 'I don't want to rush you.'

'That's ample,' said Ms Minola briskly, clutching a bunch of white roses. 'I'll meet you back here.'

Will watched his neighbour stride across the graveyard, guided by the map from his grandad's file. Ben and Ani headed towards his dad. Will and Mary just stood, looking a little lost.

'Erm,' said Mary awkwardly. 'I don't actually know where he – where Dad – is?' she said sheepishly. 'As I wasn't at the funeral.'

Will felt a stab of anger as he thought of Claude mopping up all the sympathy for their father while his mum cleaned his house. It wasn't fair. It all just wasn't fair.

They worked their way through the rows of graves until a familiar name jumped out from the stones:

HERE LIES REX DAVENANT

BORN AND DIED 23RD APRIL

BELOVED FATHER,
GRANDFATHER AND FRIEND

'He died on his birthday?' was Will's first thought.

'I told you Dad liked things to be neat and tidy,' Mary said quietly.

Will had to swallow down the warm anger in his throat. Rex Davenant hadn't been a beloved anything to him and his mum. He had been a useless waste of—

A soft sobbing next to him stopped his raging.

His mum was crouched over the grave. And she was desperately weeping.

'Oh, Papa,' she cried. 'Why?'

Will had no answer for her. He had too many questions of his own.

So he did the only thing he could.

He knelt down and he put his arms around his mum.

They stayed like that for he didn't know how long. He thought of Rex and he thought of his dad. He thought of Bianca and of Ani's mum. So many people who should have been there with them. Such a sad space where they should have been. Eventually, Mary's tears cried themselves out and she brought Will's hand to her lips.

'Thank you,' she said, wiping her eyes and smiling at her son. 'I needed that. Let's go and meet the others.'

Will swallowed down the bitter words on his lips. Mary didn't need to cry over her father's grave. She'd needed a father to wipe her tears. There had been so many over recent years.

They were just heading back towards the church, when Will spotted Ms Minola, standing at Bianca's grave. He looked at his mum.

'Do you mind if I . . .' he began.

His mum looked over at the lonely figure.

'Of course,' she said. 'Take all the time you need.'

Will accepted the squeeze to his hand and made his

way towards his neighbour, who was staring blankly at the gravestone.

'They called her Perdita,' she said, pointing to the name on the grave. 'Her new family. I like it.'

'I like Bianca better,' said Ani, coming to join them.

'It's strange,' said Ms Minola eventually. 'I thought I'd feel . . . something. Anything. Everything. But I don't. I don't know this Perdita. She's not my child. Does that make me awful?'

Will didn't know what to say. But Ani did. And this time, he was glad of it.

'I think it makes you human,' she replied. And she was absolutely right.

'She would have been fifty today,' Ms Minola sighed. 'A grown woman. And I never even knew the child. Why didn't Rex tell me?'

Will had few good things to say about his grandfather. But he was prepared to defend him on this.

'I think maybe he thought the hope was better,' he proffered.

'Maybe he was right,' Ms Minola sighed. 'Maybe he was not. Is there ever a good time to tell someone something they don't want to hear?'

Will felt a stabbing pang in his guts. The number of times he'd asked himself the same question . . .

They stood in respectful silence for some, or maybe

many, moments, each with their own thoughts. Will thought of Ms Minola never meeting her daughter. And of Ani, never meeting her mother. Was it better to have known and loved his dad than never to have met him? Was losing someone easier or harder than never knowing them at all? Or did loss have no value? Was it just its own unmanageable weight? These weren't easy questions. And they had no easy answers.

Will wasn't a great one for touching. He found human contact to be a complicated and confusing idea. It could be so very good. Or it could be so very awful.

So no one was more surprised than him when he found himself reaching out to hold Ms Minola's hand.

Will didn't have the words to give his friend.

But he hoped this drew the picture for her.

He felt Ms Minola's fingers curl around his and saw her other hand reach for Ani's. And there they stood. A childless mother. A motherless daughter. And a boy without his father. Half the people. With twice the love.

'Come on,' said Ms Minola wearily. 'Let's go. I've done what I came here to do, it's time to—'

'Excuse me?' came an enquiring voice behind them. 'I don't mean to intrude . . . Are you a friend of Perdita's?'

They turned around to find a young woman standing behind them – no more than thirty, Will guessed. He'd never seen her before. And yet there was something incredibly familiar about her.

Ms Minola let out a deep, sad breath.

'No,' she said quietly. 'I didn't know Perdita at all.'

Will watched the younger woman's shoulders drop in disappointment.

'Ah,' she said, laying a bunch of sunflowers on the grave. 'Sorry to trouble you.'

Ms Minola smiled politely and started to walk away.

'Erm, Ms M?' Ani urged. 'Don't you want to know who that was?'

'None of my business,' Ms Minola replied. 'This chapter is closed. I need to—'

'It's just,' the woman called after them, 'I was hoping you might be able to tell me something about her? I know so little.'

Ms Minola stopped and turned to face the young woman with a sad smile.

'Me too,' she said sadly. 'All I can say is that she was the most beautiful baby born to any woman in creation. And I just hope she had a happy life.'

Ms Minola made to leave once more. But the woman's voice rang through the graveyard like a gunshot.

'She did,' she said simply.

Will watched the colour drain from Ms Minola's face. She turned once again.

'I'm sorry?' she asked. 'What did you . . .'

'She did,' the woman repeated. 'Have a happy life, I mean. At least, that's what my grandparents tell me.'

'Your grandparents . . . knew her?' Ms M asked with a shaking voice.

The young woman shrugged.

'Very well,' she said with a sad smile. 'They adopted her.'

Will's brain was whirring as he tried to assemble the scene before him.

'Hold on,' said Ani, her nose more wrinkled than ever. 'If Perdita's parents were your grandparents . . . then that makes you . . .'

'Hi,' said the woman with a friendly smile, stretching out her hand. 'I'm Perdita's daughter – not that I really knew her either. My mother passed away when I was just a baby. And you are?'

Ms Minola's shaking hand stretched out towards the bemused young woman.

'Katherine Minola,' she said. 'Bia— Perdita's birth mother. My daughter was taken from me when she was just a baby too.'

The young woman withdrew her hand and raised it, trembling, to her mouth.

'Oh my . . .' said the woman, welling up. 'That would make you . . . you're my . . .'

'I'm your grandmother,' said Ms Minola, her whole

body shaking.

A moment passed.

Neither of them had the words.

So they threw themselves into each other's arms.

After a few tear-bathed, silent moments, Ani pressed something into both women's hands.

'They're clean,' Ani whispered. 'Mostly.'

Will and Ani watched as Ms Minola and her granddaughter absorbed each other in shocked delight. They touched each other's faces, held each other's hands, stroked each other's hair. With every touch, a bridge began to build across the years between them. And it was wonderful to watch it grow.

'Wait,' sniffed Ms Minola, holding her granddaughter at arm's length. 'I don't even know your name!'

The young woman smiled tearfully at her grandma. Her name burst out joyfully through the sadness, like confetti in a churchyard.

'It's Bianca,' she sobbed happily.

As Ms Minola gasped, cried, then took her granddaughter deep into her arms, Will could see it had finally happened.

She had found her Bianca.

And now she was feeling something.

Anything.

Everything.

It was a very different car ride back to Arden Heights. Wary of her previous experience, Ben tactfully ensured Ms Minola and Bianca exchanged details to prove they were who they said they were. Bianca had a picture of her mother's adoption certificate on her phone, Ms Minola had her daughter's birth certificate on hers. There was no doubt about it. They were family.

Bianca offered to take Ms Minola for a cup of tea, but Ms Minola insisted it was something rather stronger. They headed off happily together to fill in the missing pieces of each other's jigsaws. And Will felt the world shine a little brighter for it.

'Well, that's one happy ending, at least,' said Mary with a satisfied smile as they arrived back at Arden Heights.

'But . . . why didn't Perdita look for her mother?' Ani asked. 'Why didn't Bianca? Why didn't they find each other sooner? Why?'

Ben put his arm around her shoulders.

'These are impossible questions, Ani,' he said soothingly. 'But at least Ms Minola now has some kind of answer.'

Ani didn't look satisfied. But then, she never did.

'Ah, just in time,' came Claude's voice across the car

park as his taxi pulled up to the door. 'Mary, we've done some shopping – a few essentials – smoked salmon, champagne, a new suit, some ski boots. Carry it all in, would you? We're absolutely shattered.'

Mary was about to go towards the car, when Ben stood in her way.

'You've got a big strong lad there, Claude,' he called out, signalling towards Jon. 'Why doesn't he carry your bags up for you? I'm sure he can manage. My Ani can carry twice that without breaking sweat.'

'Ben, thank you,' Will heard his mum whisper. 'But it's fine. It's easier this way.'

Once again, Will was taken aback by how much his mum changed around her brother. Over these few days at Arden Heights, she'd been like a plant put out in the sunshine, growing, thriving, blooming. But now Claude was back. And he was watching his mother wither before his eyes.

'Easier for whom?' Ben asked quietly, his eyes full of concern. Will watched his mum struggle with her answer.

'Easier for us all,' she said, going to fetch the shopping out of the car. Claude looked back at Ben with a smug grin. Ben looked like he wanted to put it on the other side of his face.

'Oh, and, Mary, dear?' Claude called after his sister.

'Yes,' groaned Mary, struggling under the weight of bags until Ben took them from her.

'You need to get Father's affairs in order lickety-split,' Claude pronounced with an obnoxious click of his fingers. 'I need you back in London. Work is piling up and the house is an absolute tip. Jonny had a few friends round for his nineteenth, the little tyke. They absolutely trashed the place.'

'Then *they* should clean it up,' said Ani through clenched teeth.

'Oh, you know young people,' said Claude, looking directly at her. 'Disobedient. Wilful. Rude. I can't get through to them at all. So, Mary, *you'll* need to sort it out.'

'Can't wait,' sighed Mary as they headed towards the lift. 'I'll do it when I'm back next week.'

'No,' said Claude firmly. 'You'll sort it out tomorrow. When you return to London with me.'

Mary stopped, looked at Will, then Ben, then her brother.

'But . . . you said we could use the flat all week,' she argued. 'There's hours of work left, and we've barely had any time to enjoy ourselves.'

'You're not here to enjoy yourselves,' said Claude sternly. 'You're here to sort out my father's rubbish. That's what I need you to do. And so you'll do it.'

Will wanted to speak up. To tell his uncle that the way he spoke to and treated his mother was completely unacceptable. To tell him that he could stick his job and his house and he and Mary would make their own, better way without him. He wanted to. He could feel the words burning his tongue. Will opened his mouth—

'Shut it, Rat,' he heard his cousin growl. Will knew how this went if he didn't.

And so he did.

Will could see Ani's jaw twitching, desperate to have it out with Claude. But Ben's arm touched her shoulder. This wasn't their fight. It was his and his mum's. And they were never going to win.

'I picked up some steaks for dinner,' said Claude as they reached the flat. 'You can cook them for Jon and me. I assumed you'd already made provision for you and William. And we don't want to waste food.'

'Stop eating, then,' Ani muttered.

'What was that?' Claude snapped.

'Nothing,' Ani said sweetly, grabbing Will's arm as a light rain started to fall. 'C'mon, Will – let's go round to mine. It's way too . . . crowded down here.'

Will allowed Ani to lead him into Arden Heights, still raging with himself for not standing up for his mum. Ani and Ben hardly knew Mary, but both spoke up. What was wrong with him? Why couldn't he just . . . say stuff?

With the lift already plastered with Angela's edicts, the hallways were now covered in posters with new rules, including a list of banned cooking smells after four p.m., the outlawing of multicoloured towels and some very specific guidelines for when to use a blender. Ani casually ran her hand along the wall, ripping them down as she went.

'You're just looking for trouble,' Will said, shaking his head.

'What?' she shrugged innocently. 'There's no poster saying I can't do it.'

She unlocked her front door and went into the living room, where Olivia was sitting, looking out of the window.

'Hey, Liv,' she said, giving Olivia a kiss on the cheek. Olivia turned to them both, her facing shining from within as she saw them.

'Hello, my darling,' she said, giving Ani a gentle hug. 'And lovely to see you again, Rex. I do so enjoy our visits. I've still got it. I'm keeping it for her.'

Will felt himself tense. It was the first time he'd seen Olivia since his confession the previous night and he was worried about what she might say – or what someone might believe. But if Olivia remembered their conversation, she said nothing more of it. That was a relief.

'Do you have everything you need?' Ani asked Olivia tenderly.

'Life, love and laughter,' came the reply. 'The rest is nothing.'

Ani smiled and hugged her.

'C'mon,' she said to Will. 'Let's get something to eat.'

They went into the kitchen and Ani made them sandwiches. Normally, Will would have gobbled his down – he'd barely eaten. But after an eventful day, he found he had no appetite.

'So, where will you go?' he asked Ani. 'If the Heights . . . you know.'

'Who knows?' said Ani, throwing her own uneaten sandwich back at the plate. 'I just hope it's around here – I love my school and—'

'Wait, you actually like school?' Will asked.

'This one I do,' Ani shrugged. 'And believe me, I've been to enough to know a good one. Before Ben I was in two care homes and with four different foster families.'

'Wow,' said Will quietly. 'That must have been tough.'

'It varied,' she said. 'Some were great. Some were OK. Some were . . . not. But Ben's the best.'

'He seems cool,' Will agreed.

'I'm glad you like him,' Ani said impishly. 'Because I think you're going to be seeing a lot more of him.'

She made a heart symbol with her hands.

'Not if we're going back to London tomorrow,' Will said. He watched Ani's face fall.

'Oh, yeah,' she said sadly. 'That.'

There was a knock on the kitchen door frame. It was Ben.

'It's time,' Ben said grimly. 'We'd better go, kids. Ani love, I know how hard you've tried. But I think we need to prepare ourselves for a disappointment.'

Will heard Ani take a deep breath.

'I know,' she said. 'But there's always hope?'

Ben smiled at his foster daughter.

'There is,' he said. 'Let's hope for a miracle.'

Will followed them out of the flat and towards the stairwell. He knew a lot about hoping for miracles.

Enough to know that they never turned up when you needed them.

CHAPTER XIX

The Ides of Arden Heights

The wet weather had forced the vote inside, so the recreation room was bustling by the time Will, Ben and Ani reached it. The table that had been at the centre of the residents' committee meeting had been moved aside to allow for rows of chairs, most of which were already taken. A frantic waving across the room caught Will's eye – his mum was holding three chairs for them. Ben smiled gratefully and they were just making their way over, when Claude and Jon swooped in and sat down on two of them.

'Excuse me,' said Ani when they reached them. 'That's my seat.'

Uncle Claude eyeballed her unpleasantly.

'Children should be seen and not heard,' he spat at her. 'Sit on the floor, there's a good girl.'

Ben gestured to Ani to save her battles and she and Will sank down against the wall. Will could feel Ani trembling next to him.

'You never know,' he tried to reassure her. 'Some people might have changed their minds. Stranger things have happened.'

'Maybe,' said Ani as she stared nervously towards the front, where Angela was calling everyone to order.

'Thank you, thank you!' she tried to call over the hubbub. 'If you'd kindly . . .'

But no one was paying any attention, caught as they were in their own chit-chat. Angela's face darkened.

'SILENCE!' she yelled over the noise, bringing the room to an immediate and stunned hush. Apart from gentle applause from Coral.

'Thank you, dearies,' she continued in her sickly-sweet way, hugging a clipboard to her chest. 'Now, as the newly elected chair of the residents' committee, it is my honour and duty to oversee this critical vote regarding the future of Arden Heights. As you are aware, we have been approached by the local developer, Egeus, who is offering to purchase all the flats before redeveloping the whole site into a luxury hotel.'

There were disgruntled mutters from those who were clearly against the development – although, Will noted, not as many as he would have liked.

'However,' Angela continued, 'should the threshold be met, the clause that prevents the sale from proceeding will be invoked. With the caretaker flat ineligible to vote' – Caleb gave a dissatisfied grunt from his chair – 'there are thirty-seven votes remaining,' Angela said, giving him the side-eye. 'So for clarity, twenty or more votes against will prevent the sale.'

She consulted her clipboard.

'I have already been sent proxy votes by those unable to attend tonight,' Angela announced, 'which brings the tally to thirteen for the development and nine against.'

'Could be worse,' Will whispered hopefully to Ani. 'And, let's be honest, the people who are voting for are less likely to be here, they won't care as much.'

'Hmmm,' said Ani. 'We'd hoped for more.'

'And so,' Angela said, raising her voice over the murmured conversation. 'I will now be asking each of the remaining flat owners to cast their vote. 'In no particular order, then, Ferdinand Navarre, flat 9?'

'I'm off on a singles cruise around France,' said Ferdinand. 'So I vote for!'

'Henry King?' Angela asked.

'Which one?' came six replies.

'Flat 37,' Angela replied, consulting her clipboard.

'I sent my proxy vote on the eighth!' huffed this Henry King. 'Thought I was going to be in Tenerife!

Typical, everyone always forgets about me. And not a chance! If I can see off greedy ex-wives, I can see off greedy new developers! I'm dead against!'

A loud cheer went up from the rest of the King family. Except for one woman, who Will presumed to be one of the ex-wives.

And so it went on. Flat 38 voted for. Flat 35 voted against. Flat 26 voted for. And so did flat 28.

'We're too far behind,' Ani said, her hands fidgeting. 'That's eleven to us. They've got seventeen already. We need someone to surprise us.'

'Flat 23. Ben Touchstone,' said Angela icily.

'Passionately against,' said Ben, to a smattering of applause.

'There's always one,' sighed Angela. 'Flat 29? Claude Davenant?'

'For!' Claude called curtly, giving Ben a satisfied sneer. Will looked apologetically at Ani, but she smiled back. She knew it wasn't his fault. It was Claude's. Like so many things that were wrong in his life.

'Oh, no,' Ani groaned. 'That's eighteen votes for. We only have twelve. We're stuffed.'

Angela moved quickly on.

'Flat 11,' Angela asked. 'Monty Capulet?'

Monty looked sadly over at the children.

'I'm afraid,' he said, 'I'm going to have to vote–'

‘Monty! WAIT!’ came a cry from the doorway. ‘I need to speak with you.’

Will and Ani joined the whole room in turning to see the intruder.

It was Sylvie.

Dressed in a shirt and trousers.

And wearing a joke-shop nose and glasses.

‘OK,’ whispered Ani slowly. ‘Tell me you’re seeing this too?’

‘Oh, yeah,’ said Will. ‘Hard to miss.’

‘Erm, sorry to interrupt,’ said Sylvie with a weirdly deep voice. ‘But I am Sylvie’s brother . . . uh . . . Wylvie!’

‘Wowwwwww,’ Ani exhaled, as Ben and Mary dissolved into fits of silent laughter.

Monty was dumbstruck.

‘You not serious?’ he replied.

‘Thank goodness for that,’ Will sighed. ‘At least Monty isn’t going to—’

‘Why did Sylvie never tell me she had a brother?’ Monty exclaimed, raising his hands to the air. ‘It is wonderful to meet you, Wylvie! But as you can see, Monty’s a little busy.’

‘Yer what?’ Wylvie replied. ‘You’re a little dizzy?’

‘BUSY!’ Monty shouted at him. Or her.

‘Well, this can’t wait,’ Wylvie replied. ‘You see, my sister has told me all about you . . .’

'She does Monty too much honour,' said Monty sadly.

'She thought that you . . . liked her,' said Wylvie, his/her voice starting to slip. 'She thought you cared.'

'I do!' Monty insisted. 'Your sister, if you don't mind my saying, Wylvie, is the most beautiful woman alive! She comes straight from heaven!'

'You what?' Wylvie asked. 'She's never even been to Devon.'

'HEAVEN!' Monty cried. 'And her jam . . .'

'Don't you mention her jam,' Wylvie gulped. 'Because Sylvie heard that you . . . preferred Meg's jam!'

Monty clutched his hands to his chest like he'd been shot.

'As God is my witness!' he said, pointing a finger to the heavens. 'Monty is a one-jam man! I love Sylvie's jam! I have never even sampled Meg's jam!'

'You're missing a treat,' said the woman holding hands with Meg in the front row.

'Wylvie, please!' Monty begged. 'Next time you see Sylvie, would you give her some words?'

'You what?' Wylvie replied. 'What's she going to do with some birds?'

'WORDS!' Monty cried pleadingly. 'Tell her that Monty only loves her jam! Because Monty only loves Sylvie! I would have lived with her for the rest of my days. And her jam. Because it's sweet and it's the best. Like her.'

Monty's shoulders slumped forward. But this time Wylvie appeared to have heard. And he whipped off his disguise.

'Monty!' Sylvie cried, snapping him back to attention.

'Sylvie!' Monty cried back, raising his head. 'This is so strange!'

Will smiled. Monty got it, at last.

'You've just missed your brother!' the Italian cried. 'He was right here.'

'Oh, Monty,' cried Sylvie. 'I love you too! And the secret to a great jam is to use preserving sugar rather than granulated! Now come here!'

She ran into Monty's arms and gave him a passionate kiss.

'Er, what about me hot fudge sundae?' Peri asked, raising his hand and looking confused.

As Monty and Sylvie embraced, a wild cheer went up around the room as the two octogenarians shared a massive smooch. It was incredibly romantic.

And totally gross.

'You came back for Monty!' Monty said, stroking his new girlfriend's cheek. 'What changed your mind?'

'I had a visit from a priest,' Sylvie said. 'I think he had the wrong flat. And it was two o'clock in the morning.

But still, he told me that love conquers all! That I should give you a second chance! That I should dress like a man to see how you really felt! Not entirely sure why now. Anyway, he was right. Remind me to make sure he found the way out, last I saw he was heading for the bin store.'

Ani looked at Will and smiled. She knew it too. So the Shakespeareans really had tried to make amends . . .

Will felt a pang of guilt as he recalled his last conversation with them. No. He'd done the right thing. They'd still caused too much trouble.

'Order! Order!' Angela shouted over the whoops and cheers resonating around the room. 'This is an extraordinary general meeting! Not *Senior Citizens' Love Island*!'

The room settled down with a collective smile, Will observing his mother and Ben sharing a shy grin.

'And so, Monty,' said Angela stiffly. 'I shall ask you again. What is your vote?'

Monty looked into the eyes of his new love, held her hand to his chest and raised his other to the heavens.

'Monty is STAYING!' he said, to a cheer from Team Against.

'And you can have my vote against an' all,' Sylvie declared.

'Yes,' whispered Ani with a fist pump. 'That's two more. We're up to fourteen. But we'll still need six. C'mon . . .'

'Flat 14. Patrick Troy,' Angela called.

Will shut his eyes. The gardening committee were four votes they could seriously use. But given how things were . . .

'I'm against,' said Patrick happily. 'I'll be staying here. Arden Heights is my home. And there's so much to love.'

He looked at Antoine, who was smiling back. Antoine turned to Will and gave him a happy wink. Something magical had clearly happened. And this one was nothing to do with Puck.

'Oh, and Rosie and Hemie gave me their votes,' said Patrick, handing Angela two forms. 'They're staying too. They've gone down the bingo for speed-dating night. They're best mates now! Hemie left Rosie a bouquet of roses on her doorstep with a sorry card, at the same time Rosie left a spray of hydrangeas for Hemie with an apology note! What are the odds?'

Will smiled again. This one did have Puck's magical fingerprints all over it. With a little help from Ariel Deliveries, he suspected.

'That's four more,' said Will encouragingly. 'We're up to eighteen.'

'It's not enough,' said Ani dejectedly, counting on her fingers. 'Even with Angela's against vote, we only have nineteen.'

'And so,' Angela confirmed. 'With only my vote left to

cast, we have eighteen votes for and eighteen against. 'And I will be voting—'

'Wait!' came a familiar voice from across the room. 'Am I too late?'

Will craned his neck over the heads of the seated adults, but he knew the voice.

It was Ms Minola.

'I want . . .' she panted, taking a moment to catch her breath. 'I want to change my vote.'

Ani and Will looked anxiously at one another. Could this be it? Was this the miracle?

'I've had cause,' said Ms Minola, smiling at Ani and Will, 'to reconsider. I want to stay at Arden Heights. I'm voting against.'

Team Against had done the maths. And they went wild.

'We've done it!' said Ani, leaping up and hugging Ben and then Will. 'That's it! Team For only has seventeen votes! Ms Minola makes nineteen for Team Against, Angela makes twenty! We've got the twenty votes! Arden Heights is saved! We've done it!'

It wasn't really his style, but Will almost wanted to join in the dancing and jumping and false teeth throwing . . .

But something stopped him. And it wasn't his natural reserve.

It was Angela.

Something about the way she was standing. Something about the way she was smiling. Will recognized the creeping feeling in his guts. Something . . . something was about to go very badly wrong.

'Excuse me!' Angela shouted over the celebrations. 'Excuse me! I think you'll find there's one vote still to be cast before the result can be announced!'

'God, she loves a drama,' Ani grinned. 'But she can have it. We all know she's voting against, she's just milking it for all its worth, she's such a—'

'I will be voting . . .' Angela announced dramatically, 'for.'

Team Against started whooping and cheering again. Until, one by one, they realized what Angela had just said.

'Wait, what?' Ben asked over the confused murmurs. 'But . . . Angela, you're chair of the residents' committee, for heaven's sake! You're supposed to be on our side!'

'Oh, my dear,' said Angela, totting up the votes on her clipboard. 'I'm not on anyone's side. And after the vote earlier in the week, it was clear that no one was on mine.'

'Come on!' Ben scoffed. 'You're surely not going to throw away this place – all our homes – because you're grumpy about a stupid vote? That's just . . . it's . . . it's . . .'

'It's happening,' said Angela with her rictus grin. 'And that brings the formal voting procedure to a close. I can now confirm that with eighteen votes for and nineteen against, as per the terms of our constitution, the required objection threshold of twenty against votes has not been met. Arden Heights will be sold to Egeus with immediate effect!'

This time it was Team For's turn to rejoice, everyone who had been sitting sulking just moments ago, now on their feet, hugging and shaking hands, congratulating themselves on their forthcoming windfalls. Will noticed that they seemed less joyful than Team Against. They hadn't saved anyone's home. They'd just lined their own pockets. It didn't feel like something worth celebrating.

But if he was disappointed, he had nothing on Ani.

'Come on, little one,' said Ben, coming over to comfort his inconsolable foster daughter. 'It's not worth your tears. We'll build a new home somewhere else. It's OK, darling. It's all going to be OK.'

Mary gave Will a big hug.

'I think what you children tried to do was amazing,' she said, reaching a hand out to Ani. 'And look at all the good you did. You've helped Ms Minola find her family. Monty has found love. The gardeners have all found happiness. These are wonderful results.'

'And the next tea dance is going to be a bit calmer now,' said Ben, as Ani emerged from his chest with red eyes and a snotty nose. 'That's nothing to be sniffed at.'

He handed Ani a tissue as she rolled her wet eyes.

'Bennnnn,' she chided, blowing her nose.

'Well, now,' said Claude, walking over with a satisfied grin. 'How pleasing. I've been considering extending the house. We need more room.'

Will tried to look at the bright side. At least he might get a bedroom now.

'Yes,' said Claude. 'I want to add a dressing room to my bedroom and Jon could use an en suite. Possibilities, possibilities . . . Well, no use dilly-dallying, you've got work to do, sister. Chop-chop, the car has finally been fixed by that frightful oik, so you'll need to drive us home and the flat will need to be cleared by the time—'

Claude – the entire room, in fact – was brought to a stunned silence by the offensively loud sound of clanging metal. With his hands over his ears, Will looked to see the source of the outburst.

It was Caleb. And he was banging his broom on a bucket.

'Right, listen up, I got a thing to say,' Caleb started, his face leering at everyone unpleasantly. 'This vote ain't over.'

Angela put down the glass of champagne she had poured herself and turned to the caretaker. And his twin brother. Anthony smiled at Will and Ani.

'Goodness gracious, there are two of you!' Angela

drawled. 'Saints preserve us. Anyway, Caleb, for the last time, you have no authority here. The caretaker's flat is a grace and favour appointment. You don't own it and you don't have voting rights.'

'I ain't talking about me, you daft moo,' Caleb said, looking straight at Will and Mary. 'I'm talking 'bout them.'

The heads of the entire room turned towards Will and his mother.

'Erm . . . us?' Mary asked, embarrassed under the collective Arden Heights' glare. 'Why?'

The room parted to allow Caleb to walk towards them.

'Now I don't have much time for most folk round 'ere,' he began. ''S'why I don't get involved. Bunch of idiots, the lot of ya.'

'Charming,' muttered Coral.

'It's true,' Caleb said back. 'Most of you don't give me the time o' day. Treat me like an animal, some. Like I'm just here to pick up after 'em. Not so much as a hello, nor a pleasant word. It's 'ard on the soul.'

Will looked around the sheepish residents, everyone suddenly incredibly interested in their own shoes.

'But not your pa,' Caleb said softly to Mary. 'He always had time – and even if he didn't, he'd make it. Checked in on me when he was going to the shops.

Invited me in for a cup of tea. Or a glass of not-tea. He was good people. I was truly sad to see the Duke go. Although I see a bit of him lives on.'

He smiled his crooked smile at Will. Will didn't know how much of a compliment being compared to Rex was. But he knew that Caleb meant it kindly.

'Thank you,' said Mary quietly. 'That's lovely to hear.'

'Sooooo lovely,' sighed Angela. 'But it has precisely nothing to do with—'

'Your father was a wise man,' Caleb continued, totally ignoring Angela. 'Wise enough to know when he'd been a fool. And there weren't nothing he regretted more than what he done to you.'

Will felt his mother stiffen next to him. But she said nothing.

'We talked a lot about you over the years,' Caleb continued. 'Your pa never felt right about what passed between you. And he wanted to make it good.'

'Then why didn't he say something?' Will cried, the words erupting out of him. 'It wasn't like he didn't know where she was! Where *I* was! He could have picked up the phone any time!'

Caleb turned his gaze to Will.

'And I suppose you always speak up when you should, do you, boy?' he asked firmly, but not unkindly. 'Always say what you oughta? When you oughta say it?'

Will felt his face colour. He didn't need to answer. No. He didn't always say what he oughta. Even when he really oughta say it.

'Well, then,' said Caleb, taking his silence as all the answer he needed. 'Like I say, your grandpa was a wise soul. And a fool. He couldn't find the words to say sorry for what he done. So he did what he did best.'

'Which was?' Ani asked, hanging on Caleb's every word.

'He wrote 'em down,' Caleb said simply. 'Sent you a letter. Told you he were sorry. Told you he'd been a clot. Told you he wanted to mend fences.'

'What?' Mary spluttered. 'No, he didn't! I never got any such letter!'

'No,' said Caleb, turning his steely gaze to Claude. 'I don't suppose you did. He always thought you didn't want to reply. And so did I. So I kept me nose out. But I'm figuring now you never got it. Even though he sent it to where he knew you were living. With his son.'

'Excuse me? No such letter came to my house,' Claude said indignantly, although Will could tell immediately he was lying.

'Didn't it?' Caleb added. 'Cos I reckon you'd remember it. It had Rex's new will in it. The one where he bequeathed flat 29. To your sister.'

The whole of Arden Heights gasped quietly. The

tension was pulling the very air tight.

'You what?' said Sylvie, turning up her hearing aid.

'Wait,' said Ben. 'You're telling me there's a more recent will? The one that left everything to Claude was from fourteen years ago.'

'The year I met your dad,' said Mary with a sad smile.

'Can't be more than a year old,' Caleb confirmed. 'Your father felt right awful about what he done. And he knew he weren't long for the world. Wrote a new will for you – made it all legal, I witnessed it meself. He wanted to make amends before he went. He wanted to give you a home of your own. Here. At Arden Heights. He knew you loved it as a kiddie. He wanted you to raise your own kiddie here too.'

'This is preposterous!' Claude spluttered with a mocking laugh. 'You have no proof!'

'She don't,' said Caleb simply. 'Cos I bet you destroyed that letter soon as looked at it.'

'Claude?' Mary asked, her voice trembling with rage. 'Is this true?'

Claude leant menacingly into his sister.

'Well, I guess we'll never know, will we?' he hissed at her as Ben towered over him.

'You snake,' Ben said. 'Mary, I will help you dispute the will, free of charge. I will battle through every court in the land to get what you are rightfully owed.'

'You could,' Caleb shrugged, leaning back on his trusty mop. 'Or you could let Rex tell you 'imself.'

'How?' asked Will, grasping at any straw that Caleb was prepared to offer.

The caretaker turned to his young friend with a smile.

'Maybe you reckon yer grandfather were wise,' he said, a light in his face. 'Maybe you think him a fool. But one thing you know for sure.'

'What?!' asked Ani impatiently.

Caleb leant forward with a mischievous twinkle in his eye.

'Rex Davenant always kept a copy.'

CHAPTER XX

Where There's a Will

It was a straight race back to flat 29, Claude and Jon jabbing at the lift while Will, Ani, Mary and Ben charged for the stairs.

'Keys!' Ani yelled from up ahead, her speed leaving the others in her dust.

Mary pulled them from her pocket and threw them up ahead. Ani caught them in one hand and accelerated up the stairs.

'Think,' Ben panted, taking the stairs two at a time. 'Where might your father keep something as important as his will?'

'Lord knows,' said Mary, already breathless from the ascent. 'I can't make sense of any of his systems, there are just so many— Argh!'

Will's heart skipped several beats as his mum tripped

on the stairs and lurched forward horribly. A moment later and she would have fallen face first on the stone steps . . .

But Ben caught her.

'It's OK,' he said, bringing her carefully to her feet. 'I've got you.'

Will watched Ben hold his mum gently in his arms. And he watched his mum look gratefully into Ben's eyes. And he knew that Ben cared for her. And that she cared for him. And that they were going to look after each other.

And that the whole thing was about to make him puke like Troy before the Year Nine Prom.

'Come on!' he said, pushing them both up the stairs. 'We have to get there before Claude and Jon!'

They raced up the remaining flights, bursting through the door to their floor and sprinting to flat 29. Ani was already inside, frantically searching through the remaining piles of paper.

'What does it look like?' she asked Ben. 'What am I looking for?'

'Anything addressed to Mary, or anything that says: *Last Will and Testament*,' Ben explained, leafing through another pile.

Will and Mary both grabbed stacks of paper and started to flick through them. There were copies of letters, forms, receipts, prescriptions. But nothing to Mary. And no *Last Will and Testament*.

'Anything?' Ben shouted out. 'Anyone?'

Three shaking heads confirmed there wasn't.

'Keep looking,' Ben urged. 'Rex was too conscientious to have lost something as important as this. It has to be here.'

'You can't find something that doesn't exist,' came Claude's snide and slightly breathless voice from the doorway. 'That . . . ruffian . . . is just trying to create a stink. Father wanted me to inherit everything. You're wasting everyone's time.'

Will looked at his uncle. His voice was confident. But his face was not. He was lying. The will existed. They just had to find it.

'Oh, Papa!' Mary groaned in frustration. 'What have you done with it?'

'We'll find it,' said Ben calmly. 'Just think about what you know about your father. Where might he put something as important as this?'

'That's precisely the problem,' said Mary, shooting her brother the stink eye. 'I barely knew him at all.'

An idea flared up in Will's brain. His mum was right. They didn't know Rex Davenant very well.

But he knew some people who did.

He jumped up and ran towards his room, Ani

sprinting behind him.

'Going somewhere?' grunted Jon, blocking their path. 'Can't wait to have you back home, Rat. Where you belong. With me.'

But Will wasn't going to let anyone stop him. Not even Jon. He pushed passed his brutish cousin and charged into his bedroom with Ani, her locking the door swiftly behind them. The book was still on top of the box where he had tossed it – Will grabbed it and ripped it open, bringing the characters springing from its pages.

'Good day, Master William!' Juliet said brightly, back in the forest where he had first met them. 'Hast thou forgiven us?'

'Huzzah! You're joyous to our eyes!' cried Puck, flying around the trees. 'Mine's a kebab – with extra fries.'

'Glad you're not dead,' Yorick sighed.

'Who did you kill?' Lady Macbeth enquired.

'No time,' Will interrupted. 'You keep saying you want to help me – I really need your help right now. You knew Rex better than anyone. Where would he put something – a letter – that was super-important to him?'

The characters looked between themselves in confusion.

'Why, surely you know?' Juliet said.

'Clearly I don't,' Will snapped. 'Just tell me, where would he put it?'

Lady Macbeth gestured to the book that was still in his hands.

'Where he kept all his most important stories,' she said, raising her hands and making the pages glow. 'In the pages of his favourite book.'

Will looked down at the *Complete Works*, an ember of hope starting to burn in his heart. He'd found fragments of his grandfather's story in its pages. Could the final chapter be in here too?

He put the book on the bed and tore through the plays, the pages flicking over the Shakespearean's little heads – *Cymbeline*, where Rex had put a picture of young Mary, *Romeo and Juliet*, which had his wedding photo, *Love's Labour's Lost*, which stored Will's baby photo, there were mementos from throughout Rex's life hidden in the pages.

But still no *Last Will and Testament*.

Will let out a roar of frustration. How could they be this close – this close – to a new life? A new home? A home and life away from Uncle Claude. And away from Jon. Why would his grandfather be this stupid and unkind? Again!

In utter hopelessness, Will dropped the book and put

his head in his hands.

And then the tears came.

They were tears for his dad, who would have given him everything.

They were tears for his mum, who was trying to give him something.

They were tears for his grandfather, who could have given them anything.

They were tears for his uncle, who was determined to give them nothing.

But mostly?

They were tears for him.

Will Davenant.

The sad, angry boy who just wanted a better story.

'Master Will,' came Juliet's soft voice. 'I pray thee – peace. What vexes you so?'

Once again, Will had no words.

'He was hoping to find something,' Ani replied. 'But it looks like it's lost.'

He could feel all the kind gazes of his friends on him. But he couldn't look at them. Will had nothing – in every sense. He was exhausted.

He heard the pages of the book start to flick before Lady Macbeth spoke up.

'Your grandfather never finished his story,' she said gently. 'That's why we're here. But perchance, Master

Bard, you can finish it for him.'

Will heard Ani gasp.

'Will?' she whispered. 'You need to see this . . .'

Will wiped the tears with the sleeve of his jumper – at last it had a decent use – and sniffed loudly.

His eyes still blurry from the tears, it took Will a moment to focus on what he was seeing. The book was lying open on his pillow on the title page of *King Lear*. Tucked tightly into the spine was a piece of paper Will had missed during his frantic flick through the pages. And on it was a single word.

Mary

Will reached out and took the crisp, heavy paper between his hands. There was no envelope, it was merely neatly folded in three, his grandfather's swirling letters on the central panel. He hesitated. This wasn't addressed to him. It wasn't his to read. But two thoughts were proving very persuasive.

Firstly, he wanted to protect his mum. Rex had hurt her very much – Will wanted to make sure there was nothing in this letter that could hurt her even more.

And secondly?

He just really wanted to read it.

Will unfolded the paper with uneven hands and breath:

My darling Mary,

I have written this letter so many times over so many years and yet still I don't know how to start. Your mother always told me if I spent half as much time doing as I do thinking, I'd get twice as much done. So let me do something I should have done many years ago:

I'm sorry.

So desperately, desperately sorry.

I was a proud and arrogant fool to try to write your story for you. I had already cast the characters and determined the plot. But I forgot the most important part:

It wasn't mine to tell.

Leo was a good man and obviously loved you very, very much. I said he wasn't enough for you, that he'd never be able to provide you with what you needed. When the simple truth was that you knew he had everything you needed. And I suspect, so very much more.

Having expressed so much anger at the start of your love, I feared my sadness would sound meaningless and insincere at its end. So I stayed silent - when you must have needed more love around you than ever to fill the void that Leo left.

I bitterly regret not speaking up then. And now it is too late for everything I should have said.

I don't expect you to reply to this letter. I know you must still be angry with me. I don't expect you to understand what caused our rift. But please know, when you have fought for everything for your family, you want only the best for them. In Leo, I saw a life with no money for you. And in doing so, I missed all the riches I know you shared.

But I hope you'll accept my small attempt to make amends by ensuring that you and William have a brighter future than the past I created. I want you to have flat 29 here at Arden Heights. It is filled with happy memories from your childhood and I want you to keep them - and I dearly hope create some new ones for you and your son. I know that times have been hard and you might be tempted to sell it for the money - but I urge you to consider keeping it in our family. There are so many stories here that will be lost if we leave. It gives me great comfort as my final chapter approaches to know that you and William can keep them alive. In that vein, please give my grandson my 'Complete Works of William Shakespeare'. I trust he will find a great deal within its pages.

But I am aware that practical matters must

also be tended to. I have made, I hope, sufficient financial provision for you and my grandson in the new will I have written today. In addition to the flat here, I have instructed Claude that half of my estate belongs to you, with a trust established for William to finance university studies, or whatever equivalent he would like to do. I have given him so very little - I hope you will allow me to go to the great hereafter knowing that at least I can give him an education. If he's anything like his mother, he will be a sparklingly intelligent young man. Money should never be a barrier to learning. So please let me remove it. You now have my will - keep it safe. And should you need it, there is a copy with my dear friend Olivia Touchstone. She knows, perhaps better than anyone, the contents of my heart and mind. I know she will be as good to you as she has been to me.

And so I sign off, my darling girl. These words may never find you - my cowardice is as great as my folly. But writing them brings me some peace. As does the knowledge that you are in this world. I have done so much wrong with the years I was given and wasted too many on foolish pride. But you, my beautiful daughter, are a rainbow - full of colour and light and joy. And making you feel *anything less than that will forever be my greatest regret.*

Your loving father,
Rex Davenant
(Papa)
xxx

Will got to the very final pen stroke before he allowed himself a breath.

'William?' Lady Macbeth asked gently. 'Are you all well? You've gone the colour of the grave.'

Will could feel the warmth growing inside him. It started in the pit of his stomach, radiating through his chest and up his neck until it landed on his lips as the most almighty smile.

'Yes!' he said, clutching the letter. 'Yes, everything is going to be all right!'

He tore his bedroom door open and he and Ani ran back into his grandad's study.

'Mum, we need to go to Ani's,' he cried. 'Now!'

'Ours?' Ben asked. 'Why?'

'Just go with it,' Ani said reassuringly. 'It's important.'

That was all Ben needed. He smiled at his foster daughter and she smiled back.

Will looked at his uncle with undiluted hatred.

'We need to talk to Olivia,' he said, pulling his mum up from the floor. 'Come on!'

'What are you up to?' Claude asked suspiciously, Jon moving to block the doorway. 'You're not going anywhere I can't see you.'

'Excuse me, pal,' said Ben, standing up and towering over the smaller, skinnier frame of Will's uncle. 'But we're going to my home. Where you are not welcome. Move aside. Both of you. Now.'

Jon looked to his father, but one glance at Ben's hard face told him everything he needed to know. He stepped to one side and allowed Will to pull his mother out into the hallway.

'Wait – what – what's going on?' said Mary once they were out of the flat, her eyes looking more tired than ever. 'Will!'

She stopped firmly in the hallway, her eyes brimming with tears.

'I love you, kiddo,' she said quietly. 'But I'm not taking one more step until I know what's going on.'

Will looked to Ani, who gave him an encouraging nod. He opened his mother's palms and placed the letter on them.

'This,' he said as his mother registered her father's handwriting.

Mary wordlessly unfolded the paper and read its

contents. Will waited breathlessly for her response, although he didn't need to. Her eyes told the story of every line. They widened. They creased. They smiled. And finally, they filled.

'Papa,' she whispered, holding the letter to her as Ben and Ani followed them into the hallway. Mary passed the note to Ben and took her son in her arms. Will didn't know whose tears were whose. And it didn't matter. He felt Ani's arms encircle his waist behind him. And felt Ben's around his mum. The four of them stood together, a circle of love and friendship, a safe space for tears to flow.

But there was work to be done. After a few sobbing moments, he felt Ben take his mother's hand and Ani take his. They walked silently towards flat 23. And straight into Olivia's room.

'Rex!' she said again, smiling at Will, before seeing Mary walk in behind him. 'And, oh my days, look who's here . . .'

'Olivia!' Mary said joyfully. 'It's so good to see you.'

Olivia stood up and walked over to Mary, touching her face lightly as her own smiled in a million places.

'Mary,' she whispered. 'The beautiful girl has grown into a beautiful woman. He loves you so much. I knew he'd find you. I knew he'd find his little girl.'

Will watched the tears roll down Mary's face as she

took Olivia's hands in hers.

'He did,' she said quietly. 'Papa found me. At last.'

Olivia smiled and pulled Will's mum in for a tender hug. Will had only seen Olivia as a frail older lady. But seeing her hold Mary like that, he could understand the strong mother she had been. Ben put his hand gently on her shoulder.

'Mum?' he asked gently. 'Did Rex give you something? Something to look after?'

Olivia pulled away and looked at her son lovingly.

'You know he did,' she said. 'I told you, Rex. I told you I had it. And I promised I'd keep it safe.'

She reached a hand gently into her dressing gown pocket and pulled out a folded document. Olivia handed the paper to Mary, who opened it up and read it with trembling hands. Will read it over his mother's shoulder.

It was the *Last Will and Testament of Rex Davenant.*

'Are you OK?' Ben asked Mary. 'Because this is a lot. Although I'll tell you now – it's witnessed and official. This is Rex's will. And it will stand up in any court in the land.'

Will watched his mum take it all in, before folding the paper up and clutching it between her fingers. She didn't cry, she didn't smile. She just stood there. Thinking.

'Right,' she said eventually, her voice trembling with rage. 'If you'll excuse me. I need to speak to my brother.'

She strode out of Olivia's room and Ben's flat, anger fuelling her powerful footsteps.

'Er, Mum?' Will asked, running after her. 'What are you going to do?'

Mary didn't drop her pace one beat as Will heard Ani and Ben racing after them. She gritted her teeth. And there was some serious fire in her eyes.

'What I should have done years ago,' she said, powering back into flat 29. 'CLAUDE! GET YOUR NO-GOOD SORRY BACKSIDE OUT HERE! I WANT A WORD!'

'I . . . beg your pardon?!' said Claude, emerging from the front room, his face coloured with outrage. 'How dare you speak to me like—'

Mary slammed the will hard into her brother's chest, making him squeal.

'I'd suggest you read it,' she spat. 'But you already know what it says.'

Will watched Claude glance at the title, with a look that proved Mary's point entirely.

'Our father – Papa – wanted me to have this flat! To have a home! To have choices!' she said. 'You took all that away from me!'

'Oh, don't be so dramatic, Mary dear,' said Claude with a withering eye roll. 'Father didn't know what he wanted – he barely knew his own mind by the end.'

'Not so,' said Ben. 'I saw Rex the day before he died.

He was as sharp as ever he was.'

'Let's see what the courts say,' spat Claude. 'Because I will fight this with my team of lawyers. Mary dear, you can't afford the battle.'

'Yes. She can,' said Ben, coming up and standing next to Will's mum. 'I will fight you through any and every legal obstacle you try to put in between Mary and what is rightfully hers. And the only payment I will require will be the satisfaction of seeing your face when a judge takes half of everything you have.'

Claude looked temporarily lost for words. But then he regained his chilling composure.

'This is a lot of big talk,' he snarled. 'But that could take months – years. What are you going to do until then, Mary, dear? Without me, you'll have nowhere to live. No job. No money. What are you and your little brat going to do while we drag this through the courts? And believe me, I will drag it. For as long as is humanly possible. And then I'll win.'

This time it was Mary's turn to be speechless. Will could feel the despair rising in his chest – all the more painful and desperate for the hope that had lit him up just moments before.

'They can come and live with us, can't they, Ben?' Ani begged her foster father. 'We'll give them somewhere to live.'

Ben looked between Ani and Mary, his face aching with pain.

'I wish we could,' he said. 'But we don't have space, not with Mum. And we don't even know if we'll have this home now. Mary, I'm so sorry.'

Mary smiled and shook her head, as if to say that she never expected that. She took a jagged breath and turned to her son.

'Will,' she whispered, taking his hand. 'It won't be for long, I promise. I'm going to fight – as soon as I can, I will get you out of there and we'll—'

'You see, Rat?' Jon whispered in his ear. 'You're not going anywhere. Tomorrow we'll be home. And I've got quite the welcome planned.'

Will couldn't go back to Uncle Claude's, he just couldn't. And he knew there was only one way to stop it.

It was time.

It was time to tell his story.

'I . . . we . . . there must be . . .' Mary stuttered, trying to find something, anything to answer her brother, who was growing in front of them with the power he knew he wielded. Will couldn't find the words either. But his father's voice rang in his ears.

We just do better with stories we can see.

Some people told stories with words.

But Will needed to tell his with a picture.

His heart thundering in his chest, Will tapped Mary lightly on the arm.

'I'm going to fix this,' she said soothingly, although her eyes were wild with panic. 'I promise, Will, it'll be different this time, I'll—'

Will shook his head slowly. He took a step back from his mother and lifted the bottom of his jumper. With shaking fingers, he folded it up his body and felt the sticky warm air on his skin, a relief after months of being concealed beneath jumpers, coats, sportswear – anything that hid him from difficult questions. He inched it up – but the jumper was barely over his head, when he heard Mary's voice catch.

'Will . . . my god . . . what . . . ?'

Will pulled the jumper off his head and dropped it on the floor. The hall mirror reflected his bruised and scarred body back to him, revealing the picture – the story – that he had finally chosen to share. His body was a canvas of colour – dark purples and blacks from the older bruises, vivid reds from the ones he'd received as recently as the previous day. There were outlines of fingers on his arms, the faint mark of a fist on his stomach. There was barely an inch of his skin that hadn't been painted with punches. And every single brushstroke told its own tale.

'Will,' Ani whispered. 'I'm so sorry . . .'

‘Who did this to you?’ Ben asked urgently, taking off his jacket and putting it gently around Will’s shoulders.

Will looked towards his cousin, whose usual smugness had been erased by fear. His mother followed the line of his gaze.

‘You?’ Mary said hatefully to Jon. ‘You . . . you’ve been hurting him?’

‘Oh, let’s not exaggerate,’ Claude scoffed. ‘Jonny’s only playing with him. It’s just a bit of roughhousing. Boys will be boys.’

‘You knew?’ said Mary, whipping around to her brother. ‘You knew that your . . . that Jon was doing . . . was doing this? To your nephew? To my son? To our Will?’

‘It’s not my fault the boy can’t stand up for himself,’ Claude sighed. ‘High time he learnt to man up a bit, he’s the most frightful wimp.’

The scream that erupted from Mary could have woken the dead. Will looked in terror at his mother. That wasn’t fire in her eyes. It was a blazing inferno. She launched herself at Claude, who cowered in the corner with a whimper as his sister came for him, a whirlwind of hands and feet and nails and rage.

‘Mary, no!’ said Ben firmly, putting his arms around Mary’s waist and stopping her from committing murder right there in front of them. ‘This isn’t the way. I understand it. But it isn’t the way. Ani, call the police.’

'Don't be absurd!' Claude laughed. 'What are the police going to do about a bit of play fighting between two lads?'

'A lot,' Ben said darkly, as Ani dialled up the number. 'Your son is nineteen, a legal adult who will face legal consequences. As will the adult who allowed a child to be mistreated in his care and said nothing. You wanted a legal fight, Claude. You're going to get one. All the way to prison.'

Ben took the phone from Ani and headed out into the corridor.

'Come along, Jon,' Claude said in panicked tones, grabbing his son and storming out into the hallway. 'We're getting out of here. We're going back to London. Where my lawyers will make mincemeat of this country hick and his ridiculous notions of— WAAAAR-RRGGGGHHHH!'

There was an almighty crash and some ugly words.

Will and Ani leant out of the door to see what had happened.

His uncle and cousin were lying in a tangled heap on the floor, Caleb standing over them both holding his trusty broom.

'No running in the hallways,' said the caretaker with a wink. 'I told you. Someone's gonna get hurt.'

Epilogue

The months that followed were a blur for Will Davenant. A lot of people wanted to hear his story. Ben had been entirely right. The police were very interested in, and deeply concerned about, what had been happening to him. And Will had to find a lot of words – he had to tell his story many times. But every time he told it, he found more and better words to describe what had been going on. And with each telling, he felt more powerful. And when he was eventually told that Claude and Jon would be going away for some time and would never be allowed near him again, he wanted to take each and every word and thank it for what it had done.

Claude had been right too. The legal process to ensure his mum received what was rightly hers was a lengthy and time-consuming battle. But Ben was as good as his word and fought the fight on Mary's behalf. And, as he promised, eventually he won. He won flat 29. He won her rightful share of Rex's money. And somewhere along the way, he won Mary's heart as well.

The first thing Mary did – after kissing Ben a gazillion times, much to Will and Ani's disgust – was to register her vote again the Egeus development, a vote which had been delayed while there was a dispute over who actually owned flat 29. But once it was beyond a doubt, Team Against had its twenty votes and the development was cancelled. The most hardcore of Team For decided to sell their flats anyway and Will wasn't particularly sorry to see them go. Especially Angela, who was voted off the residents' committee when Julian discovered he had recorded their entire conversation about the subscriptions on the phone in his pocket. She sloped off to live with her sister in Glasgow and was never heard from again. Good riddance.

Because Arden Heights was now Will's home. And only people who really loved it deserved to be there.

But there were some absences that Will did miss.

The days after Claude and Jon's arrest had been such a blur, he hadn't had time to check in on the Shakespeareans. But when he finally did and he opened the *Complete Works* to thank them . . .

They had gone.

Most of him was happy. Rex hadn't finished his story, but Will had done it for him. And he'd found the words to tell his own. He had done his duty as the Bard. And now all the Shakespeareans were free – and they could share their stories far and wide, just like everyone should. No small part of him, though, would miss them too. They livened the place up. Not that Arden Heights was ever likely to become dull . . .

He had placed the *Complete Works* in pride of place on the new bookshelves in their front room. It was part of his family's story. It might have lost its enchantment. But it would never lose its magic.

'Budge up,' said Ani as they tried to squeeze another chair around the flat 29 dining-room table on Christmas Day. 'Ms Minola's bringing Bianca, and Anthony said he's going to come round to join Caleb for Christmas pudding.'

'Where are they going to sit?' Will groaned.

'Put him next to Monty and Sylvie – they spend most of their time all over each other since they got married,' Ani said, making a vomit sign with her fingers. 'They'll only need one chair between them – those two are like teenagers.'

'Plenty of that going around,' said Will, hearing his mum and Ben giggling in the kitchen as they prepared the turkey. 'They're going to be even worse at Mum's fortieth party next week.'

'Did you see this?' said Ani, pulling a postcard out of her pocket. 'It's from Antoine! The gardening committee are having a lovely time on their senior citizens' cruise. Tea dances every day, apparently.'

'Hope they've got some tango lined up,' said Will, reading of Patrick, Antoine, Rosie and Hemie's adventures together.

'Right, get a shift on,' said Ani. 'We've got to be down there in fifteen minutes.'

'Remind me again why we are going swimming in the sea on Christmas Day?' Will asked.

Ani shrugged.

'Because we can,' she said. 'And loads of our mates from school will be down there, it'll be fun. Although these will have to go . . .'

Ani pulled at the matching family Christmas jumpers Mary had insisted they all wear. Will pulled his off and flung it over the sofa. He hadn't worn a jumper in months. He was happy in his T-shirts.

'You ready?' Mary asked, appearing in the doorway holding a pile of towels.

'No,' Will grinned, rolling his eyes.

'Tough,' said Ani, throwing a towel at him. 'Last one in the sea's a dry turkey!'

Laughing, they all ran out into the sunny December cool and through the Arden Heights gardens. Mary took Ani's hand as they danced across the grass, Ben winking at Will as they sprinted to get a head start on the girls. The Christmas Day swim was a popular local tradition and as they reached the beach, many of the residents of Arden Heights were standing on the shore, wrapped up in winter woollens, holding flasks of hot tea.

'You coming in?' Will called to Caleb as he raced to the shoreline.

'Don't you go leaving wet footprints on my floor!' Caleb shouted back with a wink, as Monty and Sylvie stopped snogging long enough to wave at them. So many of their neighbours were there – generations of Kings were fighting over an inflatable horse, Ms Minola was chatting with Julian, Peri was happily eating a jam sandwich – they had become so much more than neighbours over the months.

They had become friends.

As had another small group, standing to one side. Will smiled. They weren't from Arden Heights. Not any more. But they were his friends too. And he'd hoped he would see them again.

'I'll be back in a second,' he said to Mary, as he approached the gathering with a grin.

'Master William!' the young woman exclaimed, no

longer fifteen centimetres high. 'Forsooth we are glad to see you!'

'Juliet,' he grinned. 'Yorick?!'

He smiled at the skeletal young man in front of him, who looked mournfully back at him.

'Enjoy me while I last,' he moaned.

'Hey, Puck,' he said, exchanging a high five with the smiling youth before him. 'How's it going?'

'Verily I thrive, real life's a treat!' cried Puck, jumping in the air, but landing straight back down on the sand again – he was clearly used to flying. 'There's joy and fun – and so much to eat!'

'Happy for you,' Will grinned. 'Lady M, you staying out of trouble?'

'Mind your tongue, knave,' she said with a glint in her eye. 'And you're only in trouble if you're caught.'

'It's so good to see you guys,' he said. 'I need . . . I really need to thank—'

'Peace, young bard,' said Lady Macbeth. 'It is we who owe you thanks. You set us free.'

Will smiled at the colourful characters who had taught him so much about the value of stories.

'I think we set each other free,' he said. And he meant it.

'Oh, forsooth, come here,' said Juliet tearfully, pulling him in for a hug, which the others enthusiastically joined.

'Listen,' said Will, aware that Mary was looking over curiously. 'I'd better get going. But don't be strangers, hey? Come and see me.'

'Forsooth – some stories must not end,' said Puck, trying and failing again to take flight. 'And you'll forever be our friend.'

'With all our love,' said Juliet, blowing a kiss.

'Don't die,' Yorick moaned.

'And behave yourself,' Lady M said. 'After all. We know where you live.'

Will laughed and turned to head back to the shore.

'Master William,' Lady Macbeth called after him. He turned to face her. 'Your grandfather would have been so very proud of you. Fare thee well, young bard.'

Will could feel the tears come to his eyes. But these were different. They were warm. They were soft. And they were happy.

'Fare thee well,' he called back. And he ran back to his family.

Ani and Ben were already wading into the sea, Ben squealing at the freezing water as Ani splashed him mercilessly.

Will felt Mary walk up behind him and throw her arms around his neck.

'You ready?' she asked as they shivered on the shore in their swimwear.

'I am,' Will smiled, feeling the salty air embrace his skin.

'Then let's go!' cried Mary, the flame burning brightly in her eyes as she took his hand and ran side by side with him into the ocean, where Ben, Ani, their friends at Arden Heights, a world of adventure and a bright new future were waiting.

Because it was time to turn the page.

It was time for a new story.

All's Well That Ends Well

A Note from One Scribe to Another . . .

Hey, Will,

Is it OK if I call you Will? Do you prefer Mr Shakespeare? William? Big Bad Billy? W-Shakes? Just let me know, 'K – thanks, babe.

I hope this finds you really well – or at least as well as someone who has been dead for over four hundred years can be. I just wanted to drop you a line to say that I hope you don't mind me having a bit of fun with you and your stories in this book. It is done with the greatest of respect (trust me, I've had to have a similar word with a *lot* of ancient gods) and because I'm a seriously massive fangirl. For realz. Like – mega, enormo-fan of the highest order. I've wanted to write a book in the world of your work for a long time. But I needed my story to be in the right place too.

So first of all – great job. Seriously, well done. It's very hard to keep a book in print these days and your *Complete Works* is still selling pretty well, I understand. Thirty-eight plays, 154 sonnets, a bunch of poems – that must have been pretty tiring. This is my eighteenth published book and I'm already exhausted – I don't know how you did it. I have made sure every single one of your plays is referenced in this story somewhere – can you spot them all? The mead is on me, if you can.

I also wanted to just check we're cool. I'm aware that there is a ginormo question mark over whether or not you really were William Davenant's dad and I don't want to be throwing shade on one of my idols. But I hope that you of all people understand that sometimes you have to tickle the truth a bit to tease out a good story.

And I really hope that some of the brilliant readers reading this story might go and seek out some of yours. The originals are sensational – but there are lots of modern translations and loads of films that are based on your work: *West Side Story*, *The Lion King*, *10 Things I Hate About You* (ask a grown-up in their forties), *Forbidden Planet* (ask a grown-up in their nineties) are just a few of the classic films inspired by your tales. Even today, people are constantly using your stories as inspiration for theirs. I guess because we still care about all the same things you did: love, identity, power, loss, hope . . . The way we tell our stories might have changed a bit since you were prancing around the Globe in your tights. But the stories themselves haven't changed that much at all. And that, my friend, is the mark of a great writer.

So, well done, Will, I take my hat off to you (with that baldy head of yours, you might need it). Thank you for letting me be the Bard for a bit. And thank you for the stories.

Squishy hugs and armpit farts,

Maz Evans

xxx

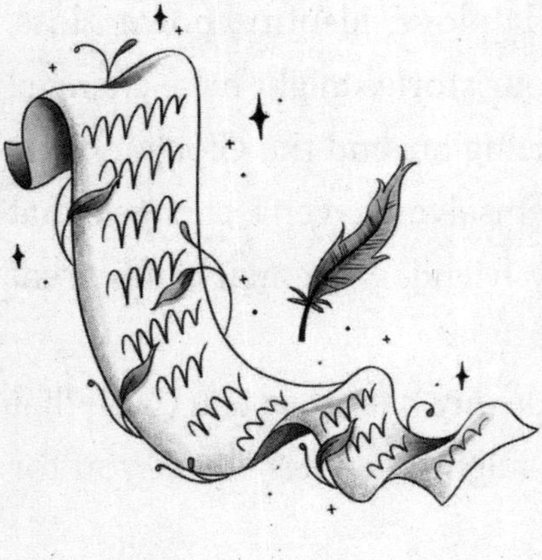

Thanks, and Thanks, and Ever Thanks . . .

Hello my lovelies!

Well, I'm not going to lie – I've loved this one! This book has been germinating in my soul for a while now and I can't tell you how happy I am to bring it into the world. As ever, I'm the least useful part of that process, so I must give massive thanks to all those who help to bring my stories to life.

Verily, the House of Chickens are merry souls indeed and I'm forever in awe of their passion, love and commitment to telling tall tales. This is our tenth year together and we have quite the history now – and rather more comedies than tragedies, I hope. To Barry, Rachel Hachel, Elinor, Jazz, Esther, Ruth, Laura, Jenny and Emily, thank you, from the heart of my Bottom for all that you have done for me.

Speaking of Bottoms, there can be none bigger than my Day One, Ride or Die editor, Rachel Leyshon. We've had some laughs, haven't we?! Well, I have anyway. You are Lady Macbeth indeed, always encouraging me to bolder and more daring plots – with the ever-present threat of murder in the air. There is so much I could say to you – for ten years you've been a total menace: fussy, pedantic, argumentative, picky . . . But instead I'll probably say the one thing I don't already tell you on a daily basis: thank you. You built the stage upon which all my stories have been set and I will always love you to bits for it. You are my Globe, Leyshy. And I think the world of you.

Every protagonist needs a wise advisor on their adventures – and for that I have my incredible agent, Veronique Baxter. Thank you, V, for your constant counsel and support. My story would have had a very different ending without you. You are the best.

This book is dedicated to my wonderful friend, Tim Sutton, who has been my trusty companion these many years. You are always there for me, darling Tim, especially during times when the pages have been flicking rather faster than I could keep pace. Thank you for your love and friendship. I can't wait to watch our stories unfold.

I have had the privilege of creating hundreds of characters in my career to date – but I will never make any finer than the three little stars with whom I share my life, heart and home. Kids – you are my greatest creations and my favourite stories. You and your daddy are the spine to my novel and hold all my pages together. I love you without measure (for measure).

The Last Bard coincides with a new chapter in my life

and one that has taught me more about the importance of stories than ever. How vital it is that we speak up when we need to, or stay quiet when others need theirs to be heard. How we must always be the lead character in our tale and not let anyone else control our narrative. The importance of knowing who are the heroes and who are the villains – and that each can be disguised as the other. And crucially, that while our stories have no first draft, you can always edit them to make them better. I urge you, friends, young and unyoung, to make sure that, no matter what, your own tale is the very best it can be. You are all heroes. And the world needs to hear your story.

Sending you love, and other things that make great stories,

Maz

xxx

If you need to talk to someone, or are affected by the topics in this book, the below organizations can help.

Childline (UK): call 0800 1111
Childline (Ireland): 1800 66 66 66
Kids Helpline (Australia): call 1800 55 1800
Youthline (New Zealand): call 0800 37 66 33